A CREED
BEFORE THE CREEDS

R. Way-Rider

A CREED
BEFORE
THE CREEDS

by

H. A. BLAIR, M.A., B.D.(Oxon)
Vicar of St. James, Southbroom, Devizes
and Canon of Salisbury

LONGMANS, GREEN AND CO
LONDON . NEW YORK . TORONTO

LONGMANS, GREEN AND CO LTD
6 & 7 CLIFFORD STREET LONDON W1
BOSTON HOUSE STRAND STREET CAPE TOWN
531 LITTLE COLLINS STREET MELBOURNE

LONGMANS, GREEN AND CO INC
55 FIFTH AVENUE NEW YORK 3

LONGMANS, GREEN AND CO
20 CRANFIELD ROAD TORONTO 16

ORIENT LONGMANS LTD
CALCUTTA BOMBAY MADRAS
DEHLI VIJAYAWADA DACCA

1003073301

T

First published 1955

PRINTED IN GREAT BRITAIN BY
LATIMER, TREND AND CO. LTD. PLYMOUTH

PREFACE

WHAT is the Christian faith? Is there a 'form of sound words' on which Christians can agree, and which will also convey some meaning to the outside world? Often enough the points on which the Churches disagree seem trivial and meaningless to outsiders; they are questions of organization and the ministry, or attempts to define the indefinable.

Our present creeds are catalogues of statements and definitions easily misunderstood. Most scholars agree that earlier creeds were more positive—confessions rather than creeds: in them they confessed what they did believe, and were less anxious to keep out heretics. The later creeds served as a fence to guard the truth and shut out error: often they guarded it too well and shut out great Christians whose thought was orthodox but whose terms were unconventional.

The earliest of our present creeds, the Apostles' Creed, did not take final shape until several centuries had passed. What form of confession had the Church used before that? No settled form, we are told—and this is a hard thing to believe. The fifth-century fathers tell us that the early creed was secret; and if they are right we should seem to be no better off, for if the creed was never written we shall obviously find no record of it. But it may have been secret in another sense: it may have been in such terms as only Christians would understand: it may have sounded inoffensive enough and yet have contained the essentials of the faith.

My purpose is to shew that there was in fact such a creed in the early Church and that it survived until well into the second century. Its pattern is seen in the New Testament and the early writings: it is both positive and relevant. It is centred on Christ and covers the great doctrines which belong to Christianity and no other religion: it is uncompromisingly supernatural, slightly

v

cryptic in its terms, poetic in form: it is also curiously in tune with trends in present-day psychology, particularly that of Dr. C. G. Jung. There are answering echoes in primitive religion; there are prototypes of its pattern in the Old Testament and Rabbinic exposition. In it Christians confessed the Incarnation, the Atonement, the mastery of evil, the universal offer of security, the fulfilment of man's highest dreams.

This is a creed which is alive and exciting, far from precise—for it deals with life in two elements. It confesses belief in a God who acted in Christ, and a Christ who acts in His Church today. It is not concerned with what God *is* in His own Being; the early Church left that to later enquirers—often less discreet. What Christians know of God (and other religions do not know) they know through Christ the Mystery, confessed in this creed before the creeds.

This may seem a slender volume to introduce so important a theme. But it has taken eight years to write—and rewrite: and in the last part of the eight years it has lost a lot of weight. A year or two ago it was an impressive mass of typescript, bristling with Greek quotations, most pages supported on a platform of footnotes. In that shape it was read by the kindest of friends, the Rev. H. G. Green, of Christ Church, Warminster, who advised a rearrangement of the New Testament and patristic evidence, and added many useful comments. After this it was read by a Roman friend, Mr. Theodore Westow, who made a number of valuable suggestions and a final series of shattering remarks: 'I think this is important. If I were you I should cut out half the quotations and all the Greek, and rewrite it all in lecture form. And' (here with a disarming smile) 'why not cut out the first chapter altogether? Anyone can write about wonder and search.' And then he added: 'There is very little in it which Catholics would quarrel with.'

Under pressure from my wife I took his advice, and deserted my family and parish for Oxford, where my cousin Mrs. Jeffreys gave me hospitality, and the Bodleian reading room provided warmth and silence and the most comfortable working atmosphere in the world. After a fortnight the manuscript had shrunk considerably and all footnotes and Greek were gone.

The result was marvellously deciphered and typed by Mr. Peter Lynn Brewer of Wickford, Essex. To all these whom I have mentioned I am most grateful.

Nor to them only: my kind family helped me much with comments and silences. My younger son's remark was the most direct: 'Daddy, wouldn't it be better if you wrote a steam-roller-man story?' My wife and daughter helped me in correcting proofs and my elder son in correcting typescript; and I am most grateful to my wife for the dust-cover design.

The late Chancellor C. T. Dimont, of Salisbury, gave me an early piece of encouragement. We met at the sixpenny second-hand bookstall which appears in Chapter 1, and he asked what I was working on. I told him—1 Timothy 3: 16. 'Ah, yes,' he said, '*homologoumenōs*. It obviously means *according to the homologia*. I hope you will go on with it.' This was reassuring from a person whom I much admired.

Indirectly I owe much to many whom I cannot separately acknowledge. Their names will be found in the end-notes to the chapters, or at least in the bibliography. And I must say a word about the bibliography. It contains most of the books which I consulted, and some which are relevant but were published too late for reference except in the notes. Most of the early works of the sixteenth to nineteenth centuries I consulted hopefully in the British Museum, but found not much to my purpose. They are chiefly included as shewing how curiously attractive this verse, 1 Timothy 3: 16, has been. They are witnesses to its importance.

Acknowledgments to publishers and others who have kindly allowed me to quote from copyright works will be found on page viii.

14 February 1955.   H. A. B.

ACKNOWLEDGMENTS

I am indebted to Mrs. W. B. Yeats and The Macmillan Company of New York for permission to reproduce the second
verse of W. B. Yeats' "The Second Coming" from *Collected
Poems of W. B. Yeats*, published by Messrs. Macmillan & Co.
Ltd. (U.S.A. copyright 1924), and to Father Joseph Crehan
and Messrs. Burns Oates & Washbourne Ltd. for an extract
from *Early Christian Baptism and The Creed*.

CONTENTS

PART I. WITNESS TO TRUTH

PART II. DOCTRINES OF THE TRUTH

PART III. PATTERN OF THE TRUTH

Part I

WITNESS TO TRUTH

Chapter 1

POETIC CONFESSION

THERE is a second-hand book shop well known to those who live in Salisbury. I was passing it and had five minutes to spare, so I stopped and looked through the sixpenny stall at the door.

It was, as usual, full of good books which had been very much read in their day. The bookseller hoped that they were now worth sixpence to someone; if he was wrong they would travel hopefully to the other side of the door where the price was two-pence.

On that day one book at least was saved from the last humiliating step. A small duodecimo copy of Pliny's *Letters* with a broken cover was among the sixpennies: it was beautifully printed by Elzevir of Amsterdam and dated 1659.

The girl inside the shop assured me that there was no mistake, so I paid my sixpence and took my find to the bookbinder to have the book repaired. In due course I got it back as fit for the pocket as when it was first bound.

When I shewed it to my wife at home she asked why Pliny's letters were interesting; I explained that they give a picture of a province of Asia Minor (Pliny was governor of Bithynia) at a period of which there are few records—the beginning of the second century.

Turning to his famous Letter Ninety-seven (Ninety-six in some editions), I shewed her the account of a Christian service given before Pliny's tribunal, by some who had been Christians but had lapsed.

Pliny wrote to the Emperor Trajan that:

> They asserted that this was the extent of their misdemeanour or mistake, that they had been accustomed to assemble on a fixed day before dawn; and to recite a verse antiphonally to Christ as God; and to bind themselves by an oath [or 'in a sacrament'] not for any criminal purpose, but that they would not commit theft

2

or robbery or adultery, that they would not break their promise, that they would not refuse to acknowledge property entrusted to them when called upon: having completed this it had been their custom to separate and assemble again later to take food—but of a quite ordinary and innocent kind: and even that they had given up after my edict in which I had put a ban upon societies.

I went on to explain to my wife that the 'carmen' or 'verse' which was *recited* 'to Christ as God' had usually been mis-translated 'hymn'.

Personally I believed that it was something like the anti-phonal creed form found in the first epistle to Timothy, chapter three, verse sixteen. This at once interested my wife, who knew that I had been at work for some years on the Christian pattern of belief in the first and second centuries, with this verse as a foundation.

We looked up 'carmen' in Lewis and Short, and I was re-minded that it was often used to mean a religious formula or incantation. The oath (*sacramentum*) in which they bound them-selves had also (I told her) a second sense for Christians.

'It looks', said my wife, 'as if these lapsed Christians were deliberately using a *double entendre*.'

This made me look at the passage again. Were there any other possible *double entendres*? Theft, robbery, adultery seemed ordinary enough crimes to forswear, the sort of crimes to which rough people were tempted. Robbery might perhaps recall the sense of the second chapter of Philippians, verse six; Christians might well forswear the sort of robbery which seeks to be equal with God. Adultery also had all kinds of undertones and echoes from the prophets, and could well include faithlessness.

But then came two phrases far more significant. The Chris-tians had bound themselves not to *fallere* their *fidem*; this was, of course, a Latin idiom—*fallere fidem* is to break a promise—and would have been understood by Pliny as such; but to Christians in an area full of Gnostic speculation it may well have meant to pervert the faith (*fides* was already a Christian technical term). They had also bound themselves not to refuse to acknow-ledge property entrusted to them. This was certainly a duty made much of in the Roman courts. When a man went on a journey he would entrust his valuables (called *depositum*) to his friend for safe keeping. If his friend denied the trust, on his return, there would be a law-suit; and there were heavy penalties for a man against whom such a breach of faith was proved. None the less, it seemed a little strange that this should be among the five offences which Christians specially undertook to avoid.

Perhaps here again we should look for a second meaning; at once a very obvious one sprang to mind. The 'property entrusted' was technically known as the *depositum*, which in Greek is *parathēkē*; but this is the very word used to Timothy at the end of the first epistle (6: 20 f.): '. . . guard *that which is committed unto thee*, (*tēn parathēkēn*) turning away from the profane babblings and oppositions of the knowledge which is falsely so called; which some professing have erred concerning *the faith.*' Jerome in the Vulgate, rendered *parathēkē* into *depositum*.

My wife's sudden intuition could not, I felt, have been at fault. Here were three phrases which meant one thing to Christians and another to pagans: they bound themselves in a *sacramentum*; they would not pervert their faith; they would not deny the truth committed to them.

Besides these were the three words which had important secondary associations. *Carmen* could be a simple ode, or a religious formula. *Latrocinia* could be either plain robbery, or something more profound (in terms of Philippians 2: 6). *Adulteria* could be either unchastity, or faithlessness to God.

The whole passage must have been a deliberate *double entendre*, in which Pliny could see nothing but a moral flavour. And in those terms he made his report to Trajan, who replied with his customary moderation that Christians were not to be sought out, nor punished if they recanted, but only if they obstinately persevered; and that no notice was to be taken of anonymous information.

The interesting thing to me was the light which Pliny's letter suddenly threw upon something remarkably like an early creed. For various reasons which will appear I had come to the conclusion that in the first epistle to Timothy (verse sixteen of the third chapter), there had survived a creed form of the highest importance.

If the *carmen* in question was a formula of confession, it at once suggested four things:

(1) it was centred on Christ;
(2) it confessed Him as God;
(3) it was poetic in form and content; and probably
(4) it was slightly cryptic in its terms, which would be fully understood only by believers.

All these things are true of the seven-line verse in 1 Timothy 3: 16.

> We confess that
> Great is the mystery of godliness, who was
> > Manifested in flesh,
> > Justified in Spirit,
> > Seen of angels,
> > Proclaimed among nations,
> > Believed on in creation,
> > Received up in glory.

At this point I must break off for a moment to say why I find this verse important as a confession of faith. It seems the kind of creed-form on which the divided branches of Christ's Church could unite. It is positive; it is Christ centred; it is uncompromisingly supernaturalist; it covers the great doctrines which belong to Christianity and no other religion—the Incarnation, the Atonement, the conquest of evil, the universality of redemption, the final glory.

But all this I had only gradually realized. The verse had always attracted me, I scarcely knew why. Perhaps it seemed in tune with what one knew of the early Church: it spoke of Christ in terms which the Greek fathers would well have understood. Perhaps it also filled a devotional gap. Certainly it seemed to summarize St. Paul—and, it gradually appeared, more than St. Paul; much New Testament doctrine was implicit in its antiphonal clauses.

What began by being a rather academic piece of research into the beliefs of the early Church grew steadily, to me, more important. I am proposing to write this book backwards. No one will read it unless he sees first how important it could be if it were true. As we discuss first what underlies the prologue to this creed (the first line), and then the implications of the three antiphonal pairs, the discussion should throw light on things

both new and old. We should at the end know more about the
New Testament, more about the fathers, more about ourselves.
We should also, in my view, be able to offer the Churches a
creed on which they can unite.

In primitive religion forms of words are repeated word for
word, from generation to generation. Every man may interpret
the phrases as he will, and they are phrases which admit many
interpretations.

In the Church, too, there are modernists in all ages, but they
die; and their interpretations are oft interred with their bones.
Meanwhile the form of sound words continues; and so long as it
continues Christians are brought back again and again to the
'deposit of the faith'.

But five qualities are necessary in a creed for reunion:
(1) it must provide a true centre;
(2) it must link the known life with God;
(3) it must be positive (i.e. not concerned with definition);
(4) it must give solid security to its initiates;
(5) it must have universal scope.

At bottom, then, such a creed will be poetry, not prose. Negative truths about God can be stated in prose. Historic truths
about God's acts can be stated in prose, though they are better
stated in poetry.

But a positive faith must have poetic expression. Religion is
concerned with two elements, sign and meaning, flesh and
spirit, earth and heaven: these are themselves poetic terms and
are best conveyed in poetic form.

I shall continually resort to poetic terms, because I shall be
discussing what is commonly called the supernatural. In the
supernatural order we include those things for which we have
no scientific definitions: they can only be expressed in myth and
symbol and parable and allegory.

Poetry has come to be regarded as a kind of luxury product
which you may enjoy if you can afford the time. It is significant
that we use the word enjoy, as if its only use was enjoyment. But
its chief use is to convey truth. Primitive society cannot get on
without it. The epic poem enshrines legend and history: its date
may be some hundreds of years B.C., when Homer lived, or
nineteen hundred years A.D., when the Dagbamba drummers

still sing the drum history of the tribe. The ritual chant still covers unspeakable religious truths with a veil of metaphor. Proverbs (whose foundation is simile and therefore poetic) interpret character and conduct in an easily remembered code.

Until comparatively recent times in our own country, poetry was fundamental to life. Folk songs, sagas, rhyming proverbs, nursery rhymes, hymns, plays—all belonged to the normal pattern of living; and by their means truth was conveyed. Poetry was a kind of incarnation of truth: by it truth was expressed. Unless we, too, use poetry and its terms, we shall turn our Christianity to stone with the jargon of the scientist or the metaphysician.

But truth is a pattern rather than a series of direct statements: it is both organic and dynamic. Mere factual truth often ceases to be true as soon as it is spoken.

A creed for reunion must therefore have the nature of poetry rather than prose. Only so will it be both true and comprehensive.

B

Chapter 2

THE DEPOSIT OF FAITH

THE Pliny passage has given reason to believe that the verse recited to Christ as God was a creed-form, and that it expressed a positive faith but in veiled terms. The faith (*fides*: Greek, *pistis*) was not to be perverted; the deposit (*depositum*: Greek, *parathēkē*) was not to be denied but guarded. That was what those Bithynian Christians had promised; it was what St. Paul urged upon Timothy (6: 20, 21), using the same two words, *parathēkē* and *pistis*.

The *parathēkē* was partly guarded by being a sort of riddle. Like the statements of the lapsed Christians before Pliny, there was more in it than met the eye—more at least in the form in which it was summarized.

Clement of Alexandria confirms this in the sixth book of his Miscellanies (Strom. VI, 15. P.G. 9, p. 348) when he says: 'the deposit-in-trust (*parathēkē*) which is given back to God is the understanding and discipline of the sacred tradition, according to the teaching of the Lord through the apostles; "what you hear in the ear . . .", that means secretly and in a mystery ". . . proclaim", he says, "on the house-tops".'

But it is not, he goes on to explain, to be proclaimed in terms that all can understand. They are to select passages stout-heartedly, pass on the tradition in sublime language, and expound the scriptures according to the 'canon' of truth. For the Lord's own teaching was, to the crowds, in parables, to which he apostles alone had the key. His exposition of his own parables and riddles was handed down in the tradition of the Church; it was to be passed on only to those who had understanding.

Later tradition recognized the secret nature of the formula which summed up the faith. Rufinus, Jerome and Augustine laid emphasis upon its secrecy.

8

'No one writes down the creed so that it can be read,' said Augustine (serm. ad Catech. I).

It is not to be written: 'on parchment or paper, but held in the hearts of believers,' said Rufinus (Expos. Symb., P.L. 21, p. 338).

'That which was handed down by the apostles', says Jerome (contra Johan. Hieros. ad Pammach. I, 28. P.L. 23, p. 380), 'is not written on paper and with ink, but on the fleshy tables of the heart.'[1]

Eight verses before the appeal to Timothy to guard the *deposit of faith*, the writer had reminded him of the *good confession* (*homologia*) which he confessed before many witnesses. It was probably the summary of this same 'deposit'. In the very next verse (6: 13) he mentions the *good confession* which Jesus Christ witnessed before Pontius Pilate: that was Jesus' acknowledgment that He was born to be a king and to witness to truth (John 18: 37). What had this *good confession* to do with Timothy's *good confession*? Jesus witnessed to Himself as truth: Timothy confessed Jesus as truth. But in what terms? We can find them in the same letter, ushered in on that same note of 'truth' (3: 14-16):

> These things write I unto thee, hoping to come unto thee shortly; but if I tarry long, that thou mayest know how men ought to behave themselves in a household of God, which is a church of the living God, a pillar and stay of the truth.

> And we confess that
> Great is the mystery of godliness . . .

—in fact the confession was in the terms of our seven-line creed quoted in the last chapter, which expresses the truth about Christ the Mystery. But, be it noticed, it does so without mention of the Name or Titles, and in a form which contains while it conceals the essential deposit of faith.

The word which I have translated 'we confess that' is *homologoumenōs*. It is an unusual word used in classical Greek to mean 'by common consent'. That is the meaning given in our English versions—'without controversy'. It is not a good translation in this context, for the Christian faith was not a matter of common consent. The American Revised standard version translates 'we confess', probably following the suggestion of Dr. F. J. Badcock that it is two words not one (homologoumen=we confess; (h)ōs=that).[2] This is possible, but even if we read it as one word it is still derived from the same root (homolog—) used of our Lord's and Timothy's *good confessions* in the last chapter of the same epistle. If it is read as one word, therefore, it can only be another *double entendre*—'confessed-ly', i.e., 'as we have confessed'.

I will refer those who are not convinced about this to a later and rather dull chapter (14) on 'The Homologia' in Part III.

NOTES

[1] Cf. Rufinus. Expos. symboli, 2. P.L. 21, p. 337. Also Tertull., de praescr., 20; August. serm. 212, P.L. 38, 1058; and serm. 214, P.L. 38, 1072. Also Iren. c. Haer. III, 4, 2; P.G. 7, p. 855. Also read Dr. J. N. D. Kelly, *Early Christian Creeds*, p. 54 ff.

[2] Dr. F. J. Badcock, *The Pauline Epistles*; p. 126, footnote. The reference there should be III, 16—not IV, 16.

Chapter 3

THE MISSING LINK

The passage from Clement of Alexandria quoted in the last chapter begins with 'the deposit' (*parathēkē*), and goes on at once to explain that it is a mystery (Gk., *mūstērion*). A mystery is something to which we hold clues: it is no secret to those who can understand their meanings, for the clues themselves are proclaimed, not hidden.

Sherlock Holmes used at times to give his friend Watson all the clues to a mystery: Holmes could see the meanings, Watson could not. And yet, for the understanding of the Christian mystery we are only required to be Watsons, not Holmeses.

Everything was explained to the disciples by Jesus Christ—to them it was given to know the mysteries of the Kingdom. Obviously they had not understood the meanings of the clues which he gave them. But they had seen that there was an underlying meaning. That is the extent of the understanding required in Christians. They are not to be as the scribes, always ready to give a plausible answer—concocting meanings out of their own minds. They are to be like children, very sensitive to movements beneath the surface of language, so sensitive that they know their own understanding to be limited. Because they are not satisfied with the meanings they can think of, they ask; because they are unsatisfied and ask, they receive.

The Christian Mystery is Christ Himself, 'the Mystery of Godliness'—as we may translate, the pattern of God's will, or of true values. Christ then stands between a world of true values (God's heaven, in Christian terms), and a world of false values (a fallen creation). He shews God to Man in terms which Man can understand: He shews Man to God in terms which God can accept. His presence in either world needs justification: until He has justified Himself He is a foreigner in both.

The Bible makes it clear that it was always God's intention

to send a Person to give the world a fresh start. This Person
would shew the world His purpose for the world, i.e. the pattern
on which He had created Life. That pattern would no longer be
in terms of a law of outward behaviour; it would be written on
human hearts. It would in fact be a complete reversal of accepted values and judgments. This Person would be King, as
God is King, but not the kind of king that men understand: He
would be Servant in His complete obedience to an incomprehensible code of values, and in this too a new kind of priest. He
would cause confusion in what the world recognizes as order,
but through Him would arise a new order governed by a new
spirit. In that spirit He would rule, and conquer His enemies.

One of the passages of the New Testament less frequently read
is the genealogy of Jesus in St. Matthew's gospel. It is an interesting passage and traces Him back to David and to Abraham.

'The son of David, the son of Abraham.'

First, as son of David: our feeling at once is that this is a
curious claim, made through Joseph. Later on in the same
chapter it is made quite clear that Joseph was not his father. So
He was not the son of David after all—unless St. Mary was des-
cended from David as Justin Martyr, Irenaeus and the apocryphal gospels suppose. But the New Testament says nothing of
this. St. Paul claims that Christ was '. . . born of the seed of
David according to the flesh' (Rom. 1: 3), which may well mean
legally of the seed of David. But in the second epistle to Timothy
(2: 8), 'Remember Jesus Christ, risen from the dead, of the
seed of David according to my gospel', sounds as if something
much more than mere legal descent were being claimed.

The two genealogies in St. Matthew and St. Luke contradict
each other, but they support the impression we get from the
whole gospel story that the Davidic descent of Jesus, through
Joseph, was never seriously questioned.

St. Matthew 1: 1; 2 Tim. 2: 8; Rev. 3: 7; 5: 5; 12: 16, are
texts which seem to claim far more than a legal descent from
David. There was an inward meaning behind the term 'son of
David' which no mere legal descent would satisfy: 'son of David,
son of Abraham' is part of the sub-heading of the gospel. He was
of the seed of David according to St. Paul's (probably) gospel.
He held *the key* of David because he was holy and true; he was

himself '*the root* of David'—again 'the root and offspring, the bright, the morning star' bringing in a new day.

When we look at the genealogy itself in St. Matthew, there is a significant comment about the birth of Solomon. David was his father by another man's wife. This is the evangelist's recognition of the rot which seemed to set in after David.

David was the man 'after God's own heart', the shepherd of his people. But, like every man before him and since, he took a wrong turning, and the royal seed was passed on by an adulterous union. St. Luke traces the lineage through Nathan, not Solomon, but he also was a son of Bathsheba. So after David everything fell to pieces, and the prophets looked for a new beginning—through David by all means, but through David by an act of God.

Irenaeus makes a great point of this. In his third book against Heresies (XXI, 4–10, pp. 950–5. P.G. 7) he expounds the inevitability of the virgin birth of Jesus. The house of David had rejected God, as was made clear to Ahaz (Isa. 7: 10 ff.) and a new birth was therefore promised in which God would be with His people. God rejected the house of David in no uncertain terms, in the persons of Jehoiachin (Jer. 22: 24–30) (Coniah) and Jehoiakim (ibid. 36: 30). A new beginning was needed, a 'stone cut out without hands'—i.e. a child born in an unheard-of manner: so Daniel 2: 34 and Isaiah 28: 16. Jesus Christ, born of a virgin, was a creation of new life, as when the staff of Moses became a serpent before Pharaoh, for a sign of coming deliverance (Exod. 7: 9; 8: 19).

Christ was, said Irenaeus, the second Man recapitulating Adam the first Man. God alone was Adam's Father, so Christ can have no mortal father: but as Adam was formed of Mother Earth, so Christ also took His substance from a human mother. In this way Irenaeus refutes the Ebionites who made Jesus the true son of Joseph, and the docetic Gnostics who denied Him human birth at all.

Jesus was son of David, then, not by descent but by act of God. David himself called the coming Messiah Lord, so 'whence is He his son' in any ordinary sense? On the contrary, He was of the order of Melchisedech, priest of God most High, whose descent cannot be named.

But He was also son of Abraham. What is it to be son of Abraham? It is clearly a supernatural birth, for Isaac was born out of due time, an act of God.. No ordinary son was good enough. In Isaac the seed of promise was called.

At David the sacred history stops short. Between David and Christ the chosen people walk in the way of rejection.[1] The voices of the prophets alone promise a renewal of the age, when the son whom David never had should be born—the new Isaac.

Meanwhile everything goes wrong: Solomon lapses into polytheism; Rehoboam cannot overcome his resentful pride; Jeroboam sows the seeds of a greater apostasy; Judah follows Ephraim into captivity; the promised return is half-hearted; the Maccabean revival becomes infected with the same pernicious dry-rot as previous revivals. But in Christ the time is fulfilled and God brings the disastrous age to an end.

This explains much that is obscure in the early chapters of the Acts. St. Peter's first speech was thoroughly mixed up with David, whom he pictured as awaiting deliverance from 'corruption' through Christ's justification at the Resurrection.

'David', said Peter, 'died and was buried . . . he did not ascend into heaven.' The whole world was waiting for the God-Man who should bring in the new order.

St. Stephen, too, began his aggressive speech with Abraham, dwelt heavily on God's choice of Moses as deliverer whom the Israelites had rejected, passed rapidly from Moses to David and there stopped short. The end of his speech was an attack on the errors of the chosen people from then onwards, beginning with the blasphemy of supposing that God's presence could dwell in a hand-made temple.

So also St. Paul preaching at Antioch gave a brief summary of Israelite history up to David, and from there jumped straight on to Jesus Christ 'of his seed according to promise'.

The age really ended with David. There were centuries of confusion while the world turned uneasily over in its sleep. The dawn came with Christ, son of David, son of Abraham, the new creature, the second Adam, the bright and morning star.

W. B. Yeats sees the second coming as recapitulating the first coming, which itself recapitulated the time when beasts were growing into men. What, after all, are the sphinx, the centaur, the harpy, the gorgon, but signs of the end of the times? The unhappy creature, struggling in two elements but belonging to neither, awaits the coming of the new creature, herald of the new age.

> Surely some revelation is at hand;
> Surely the second coming is at hand.
> The second coming! Hardly are those words out
> When a vast image out of *Spiritus Mundi*
> Troubles my sight: somewhere in sands of the desert
> A shape with lion body and the head of a man,
> A gaze blank and pitiless as the sun,
> Is moving its slow thighs, while all about it
> Reel shadows of the indignant desert birds.
> The darkness drops again; but now I know
> That twenty centuries of stony sleep
> ·Were vexed to nightmare by a rocking cradle,
> And what rough beast, its hour come round at last,
> Slouches towards Bethlehem to be born?

Something of the same numinous effect is produced by the famous section from Ignatius' letter to the Ephesians (XIX. P.G. 5, p. 660):

There were hidden from the Prince of this Age the maidenhood of Mary and her childbearing, as also the death of the Lord—three mysteries of crying done in the silence of God. How then was it shown to the Ages? A star in heaven shone above all the stars, its light was unspeakable and its new power struck bewilderment. All the rest of the stars—yes, sun and moon as well—were like attendants upon it, while its light surpassed them all. Then was confusion of mind—whence came this new power so unlike the rest? From that moment magical arts grew feeble, every bond of evil lost its power, ignorance perished, ancient empire crumbled, for God was shown in human shape with the renewing power of a deathless life. The plan of God began.

NOTE

[1] It is perhaps interesting to find a similar idea in the Abyssinian claim to have taken over the house of David and its promise, in a son born to Solomon by the Queen of Sheba (Abyssinia), Nicaule. This son, David or Menilehec, was anointed, they say, at Jerusalem, and then returned to Abyssinia with

Azaria, son of Zadok the high-priest. The Jews who accompanied him stole the ark and the tables of the law from the Temple, and took them to Ethiopia.

Since then the royal line of Abyssinia has continued the direct descent of the house of David.

(See Ludolf's *History of Aethiopia*: transl. J. P. Gent, London. 1684, folio. pp. 151 ff.)

Alphonsus Mendez accepted the Ethiopian tradition that Ethiopia gave 'a certain lively representation of the Hebrew government' (letter to Telle-zius).

Chapter 4

THE MYSTERY

WE have been considering Christ, the Mystery in the sense of the God-given link between two worlds. But the Mystery of godliness is not only the Person of Christ, but the truth about Him. His own 'good confession' was that He was King first—the long awaited son of David, King and Priest in a new order. But in the second half of His confession before Pilate He claimed to bear witness to truth: truth about God to men, and truth about men to God. Knowledge of God, whether through the Person of Christ or by some other means, demands understanding: and only knowledge of the purpose of God for man can make us understand the meaning of godliness (*eusebeia*).

Not all truth is knowable. Truth of this kind may be called a mystery, in which a sense of awe comes from the feeling that things are being signified which are beyond us. There were times in the ministry of Jesus when His disciples and others suddenly felt this about Him. Fear and amazement play a great part in the gospel story.

Mystery may also mean, for Christians, truth which is knowable but not yet known. Such truth Christ came to reveal to those who had eyes to see and ears to hear. Such truth is summed up in the word '*eusebeia*' which we inadequately translate 'godliness', and which I shall be discussing in the next chapter.

Much of the meaning of the New Testament we can best understand from the early fathers, of whom I personally would choose two second century giants—Irenaeus and Clement of Alexandria. One almost never looks to them in vain. Here are two passages from Irenaeus (c. Haer. II, XXVIII, 3; pp. 805–6, P.G. 7) on our subject:

> If even on matters concerning the created world some problems still rest with God, while others have been added to the sum of human knowledge, what is there hard in that? If also in our

17

searching of the scriptures—for all scriptures are things of the spirit—we expound some by the grace of God, some will still rest with God. And that will be true not only of this present age, but also of the age to come, so that God may always be teaching, and man always learning from Him. . . .

If therefore, just as we have said, we leave some of our queries to God, we shall not only keep safe our faith and stay secure in it (while every God-given scripture will be in tune with it—the parables will agree with what the scripture explicitly declares, and the clear statements of scripture will expound the parables); but we ourselves will notice how the single symphonic theme emerges from the series of chords which combine to make up these utterances.

There will always be new truths to be discovered in Christ the mystery, the witness to truth. We are told to ask questions and expect true guidance in the answers sent by God. But we must not expect three-dimensional answers to questions about the spirit element. Christ the Mystery stands in full consciousness in two elements—of flesh, and of spirit: flesh is the sign, spirit the meaning; flesh is the riddle, spirit the answer; flesh is time, spirit is eternity. We also belong to those two elements, but are fully conscious only of one. In the other we live by faith, and that is the password through Jesus Christ to a truth beyond reason (though not contrary to it). And faith is an act of will, not just intellectual assent.

The key passage begins with Peter's confession of faith at Caesarea Philippi. Such faith transfigures, imperfect though it was in its immediate outcome. In the surrender of common sense at Caesarea Philippi began the ascent of the mountain of vision, where the mystery is laid open to human eyes and ears. It is tempting to close both eyes and ears: the light is too bright for our eyes (we know that without opening them), the voice of God too loud for human ears. Yet if we open eyes and ears, the vision may dazzle and quiver like the sun at noon—our heads may reel and throb in the sound of the trumpet voice of God— but there will be an unmistakable rightness about it none the less. 'Lord, it is good for us to be here.'

Christ stands between flesh and spirit, always translating spirit into flesh (Incarnation), always transforming word and action into meaning (Justification). That is why His title, the

Mystery of Godliness, introduces this brief but comprehensive creed, this summary of the essential faith, this verse in which deep answers to deep, spirit to flesh, across the gulf which Christ has bridged.

The importance of the title Mystery applied to Christ is in its equal balance between flesh and spirit. The Reformed Churches of to-day lay too much emphasis on the flesh. Christ is either in the experience of conversion or in the good life; study of the New Testament is the quest of the Jesus of history; discipleship is the imitation of Him. All these are good things but belong to the flesh side of the sacrament—the outward and visible—for even conversion, known as an experience, comes through the senses. So for us, as for the Jews of our Lord's day, the Mystery emphasizes the inward-and-spiritual nature of Christ and the Church.

But for the nations about Palestine it was a different matter. They were too much inclined to an inward-and-spiritual religion which had no effect upon conduct. Our difficulty is to see that anything matters besides the good life: their difficulty was to see that the good life had any connexion with religion at all. The good life was a philosopher's dream, a matter of citizenship —not a religious affair. It was not hard to persuade them that the gospel of Christ was spiritual—that He was spiritual; the difficulty lay in persuading them that He was a real man and not a 'bodiless daemon'.

In the West, however, the emphasis was on the good life. The earliest traces of Western creeds are factual, and full of definitions calculated to shut out the unhealthy and over spiritual emphasis of unbalanced Easterns. But the factual and historical alone is equally unbalanced.

We are now in an age when we must either discover again the meaning of Mystery, or be lost ourselves. We must have a fully sacramental Christianity, and any scheme of reunion must be based upon a sacramental formula.

Sacramentum is the normal translation of the Greek *mustērion*. Jerome, in the Vulgate, does sometimes use the Greek word Latinized, *mysterium*, but he also uses *sacramentum*. The earlier Latin fathers use *mysterium* only when they mean the pagan mysteries.

But we, as a whole, are far too outward-and-visible in our Christianity: Jesus remains for the normal reformed churchman the Jesus of history. Where our sacraments are taken seriously at all, they are thought of as something 'extra'—a kind of spiritual sal volatile. What we need is some of the Quaker emphasis on the whole of life as a sacrament, built upon Christ the Mystery of godliness; an existence in two elements, and yet without the Quaker exclusiveness which denies the validity of particular sacramental channels.

Before we pass on from *Mystery* to *godliness*, we must look at an interesting bit of history. The question arises why, if this creed pattern was so important, it ever lost its importance. One word gives the answer: Gnosticism.

Anyone who has read the rather tedious collection of Gnostic writings known as the Pistis Sophia will understand why orthodox Christians disliked the word Mystery. It recurs with the sickening persistence of a passing-bell, every few lines. The Gnostics loved mysteries: where they could not find any they made them up, or imported them from any convenient religion which lay to hand. Where they found them they expounded them in terms more difficult than those they were expounding. '*Obscurum per obscurius*' was the motto of their spiritual progeny of the Middle Ages, the alchemists.

It is not surprising, then, that the Church took fright and said, in effect, 'Let us have some good prosaic theology, full of the Divine attributes, thoroughly Trinitarian, with a clear historical section about Jesus Christ.' That was not, of course, exactly how it happened—it was a gradual business: in fact the slow emergence of the Apostles' Creed is one of the strange things about the early Church. It is part of the evidence which supports the view of Rufinus, Augustine and Jerome that there was a creed in early days, but unwritten. The view that there was a secret and unwritten creed, which had (like the Fish) the nature of a password, is now commonly rejected. It is rejected, strangely enough, because there is no evidence for it. There was no secret creed because it was too successfully secret. The evidence of Rufinus (it is said) can be ignored because he made so many misstatements: Jerome and Augustine (who did not ignore it) must be tarred with the same brush.

But the Church was easily frightened away from dangerous doctrines and formulae. Even the great Irenaeus was frightened away from Christian angelology by the Gnostics.[1]

How much more easily would he and the Western fathers be frightened away from a creed known as *The Mystery*, or even *The Mystery of godliness*! And, more than that, the poetic balance of its clauses had been imitated by the Gnostics, especially by Valentinus in his system of Divine emanations in pairs.

Consequently, we find three successive phases:

(1) The period when our creed-pattern was in oral use at least in Asia Minor and the East, but not normally written down (about A.D. 60–150).

During this period we find the word Mystery freely used in a Christian sense. We find its pattern reflected in the New Testament books and in the early fathers, with sometimes an echo of its phrases or its rhythm; but we never find it quoted in full again.

(2) The period when it was regarded as dangerous, because of heretical (and particularly Gnostic) misuse (about A.D. 175–325).

During this period the verse 1 Timothy 3: 16, has only one echo in genuine writings of the fathers before Nicaea, though it seems to ask for quotation. The word mystery is used only in a pagan sense. And there is a general avoidance of the rhythm and pattern of the verse.

(3) The period when the Gnostic danger had passed (after Nicaea).

In this period we find the verse creeping back into the margins of earlier or contemporary texts (Dionysius of Alexandria, Athanasius). And we very soon find it quoted *in extenso* and expounded (e.g. by Chrysostom; *vide infra*).

Meanwhile it may well be said 'This sounds plausible enough: but is there any evidence beyond the internal evidence in the fathers?'

There are in fact two pieces of evidence, both from Eusebius. In the first passage Eusebius is giving some account of the Gnostic, Menander, and he says: '[Menander] was so eager to misrepresent *the great mystery of godliness* (*theosebeia*) in the interests of sorcery' (H.E. III, 26, 4, P.G. 20, p. 272).

The second passage is in a letter from Malchion and the pastors of Antioch to Dionysius, Bishop of Rome: in it they are complaining of the misdeeds of Paul of Samosata; one of their complaints is that he: 'burlesqued *the mystery*' (H.E. VII, 30, 16. P.G. 20, p. 716). If it were not for the first passage, we might doubt whether the second passage referred to our creed pattern: as it is, it is most probable that it does.[2] It looks as if *The Mystery* had become the accepted name for that creed-pattern in the East. Two heretics at least found it easy to misuse.

I opened this chapter with Irenaeus. I will close with Chrysostom's classic exposition of *mystery* in the homilies on the Pastoral epistles (P.G. 62, p. 554):

> Meditate upon the mystery and shudder. You possess it. Indeed it is a mystery, and great, and a mystery of godliness, and obtained by confession (homologoumenōs) not by search: it is not to be obtained by intrigue . . . (p. 555). See how everywhere he (St. Paul) calls the dispensation on our behalf a mystery; and rightly so; for it is not obvious to all men—I will go further, it is not even obvious to angels. How could it be, since it was shown through the Church? That is why he says, 'By our confession it is great'. Even in the realm of reality it is great. For man became God, and God became man; man was seen sinless; man was received up; he was proclaimed in creation. With us the angels saw him. A mystery indeed! Yet let us not make a parade of the mystery; let us not thrust it forward everywhere; let us live worthy of this mystery.
>
> Those who are entrusted with the mysteries are great ones. If a king entrusted us with a 'mystery', tell me, would we not take it as a great mark of his favour? This is it, then—God entrusted His Mystery to us; and as if we had not received so great a favour, we are ungrateful to our benefactor. We may well shudder that we should still be so blind to the meaning of what He has given us. It is a mystery which all know—or rather which all did not know until now, but which is now open to everyone.

It is a mystery, but not for the ordinary mystery-monger; its outward sign will be a worthy life; but it is not the sort of mystery a man can *know about*. It is on a different plane of revelation, and is known to be valid because of the Person from whom it comes. Like the truths which are the pre-suppositions of all life, it is self-authenticating. It is something like the '*gnosis eusebeias*' of Philo—the certainty of what the good life is—the categorical imperative. It is the quality which gives the Christian sense to faith.

NOTES

[1] See my article in the *Church Quarterly Review* (vol. CLII, p. 141), 'Two Reactions to Gnosticism'.

[2] Both these quotations from Eusebius have one eye on our creed pattern, and the other on the Eucharist. There is no doubt, as will be seen, that the mystery-creed is linked very closely with the Mysteries—or, as we more usually call them, the Sacraments. The Pliny quotation (ch. 1) shewed Christians 'reciting the verse to Christ as God' at what must have been the early Eucharist; at which there may sometimes have been the sacrament of Baptism too.

Menander was misrepresenting the mystery not only by misuse of the mystery-creed, but by making magic of the Eucharist of which Christ the Mystery was the centre. Indeed the pattern of the mystery-creed is very close to the pattern of the whole Eucharist, and in those early days may well have been closer.

Paul of Samosata again was burlesquing not only the creed-pattern but the whole Eucharist. The whole paragraph in which the phrase occurs says in effect that they, the pastors of Antioch, might have been able to set Paul of Samosata on the right course again, if he had only been a man of a 'catholic' way of thinking; but they did not think it worth wasting words over a fellow who burlesqued the mystery and made a parade of it in the fashion of the heresy of Artemas. The word they use for 'making a parade of it' is nearly the same as that used by Chrysostom in the famous passage quoted 'A mystery indeed! Yet let us not make a parade of the mystery.' The pastors of Antioch use *empompeuein* and Chrysostom uses *ek-pompeuein*—compounds of the same word: Chrysostom is expounding 1 Tim. 3: 16, and thinking of the Eucharist: it seems likely that the pastors of Antioch had the same two things in mind.

Chapter 5

GODLINESS

GODLINESS is not really a good translation of *eusebeia*, but I know
no other better. *Piety* misses the mark. The *good life* is too vague.
Godliness is good enough if one remembers that it really means
God-like-ness; for it is complete conformity with the pattern of
the purpose of God. I say the *pattern* of His purpose, because the
word *pattern* leaves us our free will. It is a way of life and not the
following of a particular set of instructions. *Eusebeia* is supremely
the pattern of living which we see in the life of Christ Himself,
who could speak of the will of God as His very food which sus-
tained Him.

The remarkable thing about this *godliness* is that it is quite
unlike what we imagine a life of obedience to be. We think of it
as something admirable—yes, in a quiet sort of way—but not
heroic. But we find this word continually connected with the
idea of power. In the fourth book of the Maccabees *godly reason*
(*ho eusebes logismos*) is three times held up (in a rather gruesome
narrative of Jewish martyrs) as the *power* which controls.

Peter and John, having healed the lame man at the Beautiful
Gate, tell the people not to suppose that it is by their 'power
(*dunamis*) or godliness (*eusebeia*)' that the miracle has been done.

Lactantius quotes 'Hermes' as saying that the knowledge of
God not only makes a man safe from the attacks of daemons,
but will even free him from the grasp of destiny (which in pre-
Christian thought rules over gods and men).

Here is Lactantius, quoting: ' "The only protection", he says,
"is *eusebeia*. For neither evil daemon nor destiny have any power
against the man who is *eusebes*." What then is *eusebeia*? He has
described it elsewhere in these words, "For *eusebeia* is knowledge
of God" ' (Div. Inst. II, 15).

If *eusebeia* is knowledge of God, it is knowledge in the sense
that St. John uses it, and in the sense in which Archbishop

24

William Temple used it. He could never really believe that anyone who knew the truth, in the full sense of knowledge, could
do other than follow its way. It is a knowledge which means
much more than the normal Yes. It is knowledge, plus conviction, plus self-surrender.

But, of course, if we really did know that the Will which controls the universe was carrying us in one direction, we should
not be so foolish as to fight against it. And equally, if we are
travelling on the current of such a Will, the power which will
seem to be ours will be irresistible.

It is too light a thing to say, with Dr. Lock (Pastoral epp.
I.C.C. p. 44): 'We may perhaps include' (in *eusebeia*) 'the
thought of doctrine as well as of life . . . but the context here and
the use of it as applied to the life of all Christians (1 Tim. 2: 2)
and of Timothy himself (4: 7, 8), shows that the main stress is
here on moral life.'

In the first reference, however, we find it bracketed with
semnotes—a word of numinous flavour, for the Furies were *semnai
theai*; and in the second reference Timothy is urged to train
himself for a godliness '. . . which has promise both of this
present life and of the life to come'—which makes it a supernatural affair at once.

Photius (*c.* A.D. 870) is interesting on the subject of *eusebeia*,
and links it up with our creed pattern. He is quite clear that it is
a word of power, since he believes that it is connected with the
Name of Christ in which a person expresses his faith at baptism.
He believes (and it is not important to argue about this) that
baptism at the time of the apostles was given with the Trinitarian formula. But the baptized person confesses 'the Name'—
'. . . and in the mention of *Jesus and Lord* we are taught that there
is summed up and set forth the whole mystery of the Incarnation of the Word on our behalf' (P.G. 101, p. 320). And then
later he quotes the healing at the Beautiful Gate:

> He (Peter) tells them also that 'the Name' signifies to him the
> summary and confession of faith. 'See how', he says, 'the God of
> Abraham and Isaac has glorified His servant Jesus'; and making
> his meaning more clear, he adds, 'and in the faith of his Name,
> this man whom you see and know has his Name made firm.'
> Attend. For indeed the faith that is through him has given him

this full inheritance. Beginning the miracle, he declared that the Name of Jesus worked the healing. Then he changed 'the Name' into 'the faith', for this is *the mystery of godliness*. After this again he calls 'the Name' 'faith unto him', as if he feared lest his hearers should forget that he took the Name to mean faith. Then he adds, 'And the faith that is through him', i.e. the faith proclaimed by him. You see how 'the Name' signifies faith unto him, and faith, the godliness that was preached by him.' (P.G. 101, p. 324), (translation mainly from Fr. Joseph Crehan, *Early Christian Baptism and the Creed*, p. 156 ff.).

Eusebeia then is a word of power, an extension of the Name of Christ: the power is invoked by confession of its Mystery in its outward and visible form of words, with accompanying conviction from the heart. It involves conformity with God's will, but is no mere attempt at living a 'moral life'.

Besides which, no single phrase of the short creed is concerned with morals. It is as a whole concerned with a new interpretation of history seen in Christ, and a new promise which should carry mankind to the end of history—and beyond.

Eusebeia is neither piety, nor godliness in the normal sense, nor the good life. It is the divine pattern of good order and control which is held in balance by holiness. It is the strength of the strong man revealed in gentleness and power. It is the apotheosis of sophrosyne. It is indeed the Will of God. And Jesus Christ not only revealed that Will, he was that Will; for the Mystery is not parable or allegory—it is actual truth seen in the limited scope of which we are chiefly conscious, and so expressed in terms which can only be poetic.

Part II

DOCTRINES OF THE TRUTH

Chapter 6

DEATH AND LIFE

ATHANASIUS is the best balanced writer of the early Fathers on the Person and work of Christ. His Trinitarian doctrine, from our point of view, begins from the beginning, Christ Himself.

The flesh-and-spirit pattern is very apparent, in his work on the Incarnation; but the terms which he uses are *death* and *life*.

A properly balanced sacramentalism must draw the line in the right place (as has already been said)—not between visible and invisible, which is where we most often draw the line. We set men and the visible world on one side, and on the other ghosts, angels, demons, and God Himself. But the inward spirit of a sacrament is its *holiness*, which is its proper meaning in the purpose of God. All created things are, as is often pointed out, sacramental: they owe their existence to the purpose of God in their creation. In so far as they do not fulfil that purpose, they may be said not to exist. Consequently Athanasius draws a line between things which are (which come from God who Is), and things which are not.

The folly of being deceived, he says, lies in giving greater honour to things which do not exist than to God (XI, 4).* Later references make it clear that 'the things which do not exist' are more like persons than like things; they have wills of their own and definite though temporary powers. When he speaks of things *not existing*, he does not mean what we should mean: he means that they have not received life from God. 'Things which are not' have no real existence; for what is cut off from God belongs to a world of fantasy and error. Trust in such a world is doomed to disillusionment.

Unless therefore men are united with God, they form a kind of 'insubstantial pageant'; they are figures of an unpleasant dream, without permanence or security. Pagans are unhappy,

* All references are to the *De Incarnatione*, unless otherwise stated.

28

because they worship beings as dreamlike as themselves, whose tendance is a continual irritation.

In section XV, 6, he uses a phrase which sounds like an echo of a passage from the Didache, in which the Christian is told to refrain from things sacrificed to idols, 'for it is the worship of dead gods'. Athanasius has been speaking in the previous section of the destruction of daemon worship by Christ, and he continues, '. . . or if their mind had already sunk even to the *dead*, so as to worship heroes, and the gods spoken of in the poets, yet, seeing the Saviour's resurrection, they were to confess them to be *false gods* . . .' (XV, 6, Robertson's translation). The dead gods have therefore some sort of existence, delusive though it may be.

But the devil has been 'brought to nought' (XX, 6), and men have been released from his enslaving tyranny by the sacrifice of Christ; for the devil is the owner of the power of death. Jesus Christ allowed him to exercise this power on Him (XXI) by violence; for having no seeds of corruption in Him, Christ could not have died in any 'natural' way. On the cross His outstretched arms were a welcome to the *nations*: and by death in the devil's own element—for was he not prince of the power of the air?—Christ entered that element in the spirit and defeated the devil there.[1] From there He returned to heaven.

Life (in Christ) had thus made a pathway through the domain of death, touching fallen creation at every point (XLV, 3), and pushed its way back to God: and the gates were open for man to follow. The act of dying, instead of being the sentence executed upon a condemned criminal, became a stage in the process of acquittal—a milestone upon the road to Life—if it were accepted in Christ's sense. Meanwhile the devil alone is dead (XXVII, 3), and those who associate themselves with him have chosen death as a mode of existence, as against the death which leads to Life.

Christ has conquered death, and the domain of death has now become part of His Kingdom. The proof that Christ and His servants are the live people, and the demons the dead, is the defeat of evil spirits by Christians acting in the Name of Christ (XXX, 5-7); the evil spirits include the nature 'fetishes' of the barbarians and the people of the land (XLVII, 2). Spirits and 'gods' do not cast out Christ and so prove Him dead; Christ proves them dead (XXXI, 1).

Death, to Athanasius, is a condition and not an occasion. It is a condition of false existence, which he calls non-existence but not what we should call non-existence: it is fantasy as against reality.

> The gods and spirits of the unbelievers can do none of these things (i.e. works of power done by Christians), but rather shew themselves dead at the presence of Christ, their pomp being reduced to impotence and vanity; whereas by the sign of the cross all magic is stopped, and all witchcraft brought to nought, and all the idols are being deserted and left, and every unruly pleasure is checked, and everyone is looking up from earth to heaven. Whom is one to pronounce dead? Christ that is doing so many works? But to work is not the property of one dead. Or one who exerts no power at all, but lies as it were without life? as do the idols and spirits, dead as they are (XXXI, 2).

But the next chapter reminds us again that this impotence and lifelessness does not mean non-existence in our sense (XXXII, 4). The daemons have not been *annihilated* by Christ. It means, (*a*) that their power has been limited to the sphere of Time; the devil knows he has only a short time: therefore if Time and Eternity are looked at spatially, we can see that the forces of evil have been hemmed into a limited area: this means that those who have the freedom of Eternity are free of evil—they possess the liberty of the whole of heaven, and need not enter the realm of death; (*b*) that the power of the daemons vanishes where True Life or Reality is present: for (XXXII, 5, 6) Athanasius claims that the daemons 'see what men do not see'— and they *know* that Christ is still alive. Indeed they confess Him.

But the achievement of Christ has been more than merely to confine the powers of evil and set us free. He has not merely shewn us that Life and Death are opposed to one another, and so made the choice easier for us. That would be much, but it is not all. Christ the Life has again come our way. By entering the sphere of Death to which we belong, he has not merely taken us from our lower element to a higher one—leaving Death and its initiates to 'stew in their own juice'. He has actually deified

Death for those who accept Death. He has enlivened the apparatus of the flesh so that it may be used as the means of life.

Origen had seen that although things might have been different without a Fall, matter was now an essential: without flesh,
without death in fact, no creaturely life was possible.

Christ's achievement therefore has been to offer man a true
choice; a chance, not of escaping from that without which he
cannot truly exist, his body, but of gaining life for body and soul
together. It is a Redemption, and the only true Redemption,
which proclaims the message of Christianity as against any
form of escapism. This choice is open to man during his time
on earth, but no longer: and upon his choice hangs not only his
own fate but that of creation as a whole. So long as Christ remains in the flesh, embodied in His Church, so long the choice
remains to men to live or to die, to continue or to cease.

There may or may not be ways of escape; God's mercy alone
knows about that. It is clear that there is only one way of
Redemption, and that is the sacramental approach which
rescues the whole man, the whole creation over which man was
given dominion.

The creed of faith is that which announces more even than
the hope of life through death; it can be satisfied with nothing
less than the salvation of death and life together. The Mystery
which ends in glory is the redemption of man, his history and
his hope.

NOTE

[1] This comes from XXV, which is omitted in the shorter recension.
Dr. F. L. Cross, however, thinks that both recensions may be the work of
Athanasius.

Chapter 7

INCARNATION AND ATONEMENT

ATHANASIUS spoke of Death and Life, non-existence and real existence. He would probably have preferred the Petrine version of the first pair of clauses in the mystery-creed: 'Put to death in flesh, but made alive in spirit' (1 Pet. 3: 18).

This is the approach to glory, the first stage in Christ after baptism, the two elements in Communion. In the controversies over the essence and the accidents of the consecrated Communion elements—in our complicated interpretation of the outward and visible sign and the inward and spiritual grace—we have missed the simplicity of the original flesh-and-spirit pattern.

We have assumed that the spirit side of the pattern lay in an undefinable essence, and that the symbols of bread and wine are the material side. And in doing so we have made the typical mistake of our generation, and indeed of many generations before us. We have drawn our line not between flesh and spirit but between matter and spirit. Nothing in the New Testament sanctions this attitude. It is no question of visible or invisible, of spirit or matter. Spirit is not the element which stands over against matter: spirit is *matter made alive* (quickened).

What then are the two elements? Bread and Wine, Flesh and Spirit. The Bread, the Flesh, is broken and then accepted broken: brokenness is manifested in flesh, put to death in flesh. That is what we stretch up our hands to accept—and the stretching up of hands is a not unimportant part of the ceremonial. It is suffering, not explained but accepted as the animals accept it and as Christ accepted it. It is the accepting of physical life with its frustrations and failures. It is the accepting even of our own sins (and the consequent humiliation of penitence) as part of the pattern.

The Wine, the Blood which is the Life, is then taken after

Christ's way of dealing with the world has been accepted. The Life brings Transfiguration. That is spirit. Not that which is within flesh, or in some curious and metaphysical way *attached to flesh*; but *transfigured flesh*. It is the body, if you will, in many dimensions. The Spirit is Body plus Life, the transfigured water of the wedding at Cana.

The simplicity which appears in two symbols to denote two sides of the pattern is a simplicity which rings true to Christ. Soul and spirit have been curiously confused. Soul is a 'bodiless daemon': but Life is that which envelops and transfigures the justified body, which is then spirit. Pauline paradoxes spring to mind about the Christian being not stripped of his body (to leave—as the 'soma-sema' or escapist school would have it— the spirit free), but being 'clothed upon': the mortal is swallowed up in Life. So that even those who have known Christ after the flesh are to know Him so no more. The true Christ is the Christ not merely manifested in flesh, but justified in spirit. And the wine of the Communion is the life of the flesh, by virtue of which the Christian lives in spirit and in truth. Communion in one kind only is not just less than the truth: like all half-truths left unfulfilled, it becomes more misleading than a lie: it is an Incarnation without Atonement, the Cross without the Resurrection. We have died with Christ, and alas!—have been left for dead.

This is not just a hit at the Roman Church. That great Church recognizes the necessity of the two kinds in Communion, since no Mass is valid unless the priest makes his Communion in both. It is a matter of expediency which has led them to withdraw the chalice from the laity. In so doing, however, they have endangered the principle and compelled the laity to leave the outward and visible unfulfilled by the spirit.[1]

In the accounts of the Institution in the Synoptic Gospels and in St. Paul, the word '*soma*' (body) is used, which is a gentler word than '*sarx*' (flesh). In other connections St. Paul uses '*sarx*' often. But it is striking that in his discourse on the Bread of Heaven St. John repeats the harsh-sounding '*sarx*' again and again with almost brutal persistence (6: 51 ff.):

> The bread which I will give you is my '*sarx*' for the life of the world . . . ! How can this man give us his '*sarka*' to eat. . . . Verily,

verily I say unto you, unless you eat the '*sarka*' of the Son of Man and drink his blood, you have not got life in yourselves. He who devours of me the '*sarka*' and drinks of me the blood has got eternal life, and I will raise him up at the last day. For my '*sarx*' is true food, and my blood is true drink. He who devours of me the '*sarka*' and drinks of me the blood remains in me, and I in him.

The flesh is to him a sacramental symbol. Flesh without blood is dead flesh, as men without the spirit are dead men.

The New Testament as a whole does not use '*pneuma*' in the sense of a departed spirit, i.e. a ghost.[2] Unclean spirits are '*pneumata akatharta*', which can take possession, as the Spirit of God can take possession of the body. '*Pneuma*' may be abstract —'poor in spirit'—but when it is personal is never less than a whole personality. That is to say, it does not mean soul without body (unless in the idiomatic phrase 'he gave up the *pneuma*', or 'the ghost'): This does not apply to unclean spirits, which are in a class by themselves, and have been enlivened with a kind of infernal life, and whose object was to possess themselves of physical bodies: furthermore their power would seem to depend on their gaining some kind of possession of a body.

But Christian '*pneuma*' is the whole personality which includes the body and the senses. That is the essential contrast between Christianity and Vedantism. Christianity has refused to be escapist: the body is no prison, it is the instrument of spirit.

Spirit is the meaning of body, and so cannot be less than body-plus-soul. The second of each pair in the mystery-creed consistently gives the meaning of the first of each pair. It was, no doubt, because Valentinus' system imitated this that the *homologia* fell into disuse, as I have said. But however much it was imitated and burlesqued, its way of holding the Christian teaching in balance was the right way. It was a sacramental creed.

Each of our two great sacraments has its two symbols expressing flesh and spirit. In baptism the symbols of the two sides of the sacrament are (1) washing, for putting off the sins of the flesh—a renunciation, not of the world but of the world's values —the taking of a direction which points to Christ: and (2) anointing, or the sign of the Cross with laying on of hands, for the receiving of the Holy Spirit.[3]

In Communion the two sides are (1) Bread for flesh, and (2) Wine for the Life which transfigures it. The flesh pins down the communicant to daily life, as 'suffered under Pontius Pilate' pins down the life of Christ to a point in history. The spirit gives history a meaning which most historians have failed to find. The fashion is turning against the greatest historian of our time, Arnold Toynbee, as fashions do turn: but he has the heart of the matter.

But what was this justification? Has it a point in history? It has indeed, for we have it not in isolation, but balanced always by its twin clause, 'manifested in flesh'. We can find three such points in the gospel story. If we meditate on the Incarnation, we shall see the Baptism as the Justification in Spirit. It was the commission and the gift of a power which could yet only be entrusted to sinless man. In Christ 'man was seen sinless', said Chrysostom. It looked forward.

If we meditate on the ministry, the signs of the Kingdom, the teaching and the life of service, we shall see the Transfiguration: there, we shall say, at the peak of His life, Jesus was justified in the Spirit; from then onwards He looked forward to the meaning of the Exodus which He was to accomplish at Jerusalem.

If we meditate on the Cross and Passion, we shall with St. Peter see a death-resurrection pattern (1 Pet. 3: 18). 'Him God raised up.' There will be our point in history.

Perhaps, however, our meditation is on the Church. The Incarnation, Ministry, Death and Resurrection have brought to birth a child which looks too weak to survive for very long. If so, we shall look to Pentecost and the Joel prophecy. Justified in the Spirit, the Church received its meaning, when (Resurrection and Ascension notwithstanding) it was groping in the dark.

The Protestant view of justification is too small. It is not only the individual who is justified in the Spirit through an individual act of faith, which opens the channel of Grace: the Christian is justified in the fact that the Spirit is shared. The Spirit binds him closely in the texture of a fellowship which has a common meaning: its members all speak a language which the fellowship can understand. Apart from that there is no justification—none at least known to the Church. We may go further: it was only in that gift of the Spirit which launched the Church that Christ Himself was fully justified.

> Spirit [says Berdyaev] defies conceptional interpretation but never-theless its attributes are apprehensible. Among these attributes are freedom, meaning, creativity, integrity, love, value, an orienta-tion towards the highest world and union with it. The *pneuma* of Scripture and the *nous* of Greek philosophy are included among these attributes (*Spirit and Reality*, p. 32).

Most of us would agree that freedom is the first attribute of spirit. It takes only a moment of imagination to see the night-mare quality of an undirected freedom. Picture it as a dream in which there is free movement but no direction, no control and no support—such a dream must end in that sickening sense of falling which we know so well, without the comfort of a safe landing in a solid bed. If the spirit is freedom, then a spiritual afterlife is more terrible than the medieval hell—unless we have support, direction and fellowship.

The Christian view of Holy Spirit is the picture of God at His nearest to man. The Father, loving but transcendent, is not enough. The Son, God in the sphere of perception, is much better for the living man, but no comfort for the dying sinner. The Holy Ghost, God within the very personality of man—less the driving force than the directing medium—gives him a plat-form, a bridge, a corridor or what you will. In the Christian doctrine of the Spirit the nightmare quality disappears.

> Spirit emanates not only from the Deity but also from the primal pre-existential freedom, from the *Urgrund*. That is, indeed, the fundamental paradox of spirit: it is a Divine emanation, and at the same time it can reply to the Deity in terms not dictated by It. Spirit is not only Divine, it is Divinely human, Divine-wordly: it is freedom in God and from God. No concept or rationalisation is adequate to express this mystery: only myth and symbol can attempt to do so. This is the mystery of creation, and at the same time that of evil. Man regarded as a natural determined creature is not aware of this mystery; such an awareness is the sign of a spiritual creature (Berdyaev, op. cit., pp. 33–4).

That is the second horror of spirit, the second kind of free-dom. Spirit is the presupposition of God Himself—as Jacob

Boehme called it, the *Urgrund*. It is the presupposition of all
our creativity: the creatures of our spirit, whether poems, pictures, symphonies or philosophies, cease to be ours as soon as
they are born. They can be appropriated and used, even as
weapons against ourselves. The Creating God stands in the
same relationship with His creatures: He must remain faithful,
He cannot deny Himself: the support which He is ready to give
He may not give, He can only offer it. He can point the way to
the highest world for us to follow, and help us when we follow:
but it is we who must turn—He cannot do that for us. There is
no Christian Heimarmene.

Justification in spirit comes of faith. Faith is the weaving of a
recognizable pattern which leads the eye towards its object,
whether directly or not. Faith is seen not in a series of successes,
but in a continually redirected intention. The detail of the pattern may move from side to side, but there will be a continual
movement as definite as that of the ship which sails into the
wind. The justification in spirit has only once been perfectly
manifested in flesh; and that is reproduced in myth and symbol:
our own general direction is seen and maintained only by virtue
of continual readjustment to that of Christ.

The verbs in this first pair of clauses in the mystery-creed express Incarnation and Atonement. God acted in a mystery
which was a flesh and spirit pattern. But who or what was manifested in flesh? Who or what was justified in spirit? And how
was It justified?

Ultimately the Mystery of godliness is God Himself, for *hŏs*
(the 'who' which follows) is masculine and not neuter. Yet the
word is *hŏs* (who) not *theos*.[4] The Mystery of God is that which
expounds God—yet 'that which' has become 'he who'. This is
God in relationship with man; God, not in essential Being but
in active conversation with that other free spirit, Man, who,
though a creature, can yet answer God in terms not dictated by
Him.

The God who was manifested, then justified, was God-in-
relation. God-absolute needs no justification: God-in-relation
must be justified, or else He is not the Truth. This means that
the Incarnation is more than an answer to Man's urge to search

for what is higher than himself. It is God's consent to appear in Man's court of justice, the World, and there be judged by him. He will abide by Man's verdict.

At the back of the minds of most of us, there lies carefully concealed the conviction that ultimately *it is all God's fault.* If we are free, He made us free. If He punishes (in any other than a remedial sense), He is unjust. It is not we who should be punished but God. If any man altogether denies this feeling, he convicts himself of lack of reasoned thinking or lack of honesty: he proclaims a faith which is altogether independent of thought or human analogies. Few of us have any real sympathy with St. Paul's 'Who art thou that repliest against God?' The sort of God who will not be answered back is not the God we have believed in, but a Freudian embodiment of the angry parent. If God be such, and being such can send us to Hell, then (with John Stuart Mill) to Hell we will go. The God we know is the God who justified His servant Job: the God, not of the Yahweh speeches, but of the conclusion.

This is our God, who will never resort to an obscurantist reply, who never stands upon the dignity of His own Majesty, who invites questions and gives answers too simple to be understood. This is the God whose Mystery was manifested in flesh—justified in spirit. And men gave judgment on that Mystery and found God innocent. True, they crucified Him: but that was sentence, not verdict.

Consider for a moment how every element in Jerusalem was involved in the justification of God by men—the proclamation of His innocence. Caiaphas spoke for the priests, and said it was expedient that one man should die for the people: and when he said it John tells us that he prophesied. Justified in spirit. The chief priests and scribes, mocking, uttered the truth which vindicates both God and man, 'He saved others, Himself he cannot save'—the truth underlying the doctrine of substituted love. Paul the Pharisee proclaimed the Cross and Resurrection as saving truth: Nicodemus the Pharisee proclaimed his disagreement with the sentence of the Sanhedrin by helping Joseph with the burial. Pilate proclaimed himself innocent of the blood of that just man. Herod found no fault in Him. Judas, when he saw Him condemned, committed suicide. The centurion cried, 'Truly this man was a Son of God' (or in St. Luke 'a righteous man').

It has too often been said that the world proclaimed its guilt, in seeing what was good in Christ and calling it evil. Had the world done so, it would have committed the sin which knows no forgiveness. Rather the world proclaimed its helplessness. It found God innocent, but found no other way of dealing with innocence than by crucifying it. God was found Not Guilty and condemned to death.

So the world condemned itself, not God. 'What sort of a world is this?' 'It is the sort of world in which God and godliness are intolerable, and must be crucified.'

The character of God is vindicated by the Cross, and His power by the Resurrection.

In that same pattern lies the justification of men. In the crucifixion the world proclaimed its despair of dealing with un-adulterated goodness. It is a despair which all the tragedians knew. But it is a despair to which God has His answer. What the world has regarded as its last desperate expedient, God has proclaimed as neither last nor desperate. The last word is not with the supposed final riddance by death, which is the world's way with its heroes—because they are more convenient and comfortable carved in stone. The last word is not Death but Resurrection, and its keynote Hope. Goodness, judged according to men in the flesh, can live according to God in the spirit.

But Man asks a final question: 'That is all very well,' he says, 'God's ways to men are vindicated and justified in Christ. But what is that to me? How am I justified in a goodness which is not mine? What I see is God's power and my incompetence, God's innocence and my guilt.'

No theories of vicarious suffering, no ransoms paid, no revelations of an exemplary life are satisfactory. They may have a kind of logical validity, but they cannot make an atonement: their logic silences us, but it does not convince. We are men. What have we done to be acquitted of the charges which lie against us? We plead guilty because the Cross has shown those charges to be just. How can even faith in Christ justify, or in any genuine way associate us with Christ in the death-resurrection pattern?

D

It is sometimes assumed that the growth of new knowledge always increases the intellectual difficulties of belief. But that is not by any means true. The psychology of Dr. C. G. Jung has opened out a new field in something more than the mere study of psychology. Scientifically it is a new field, but it has a strangely familiar look to Christians. The suggestion is that we are far more securely united to each other and to our past than our consciousness allows us to suppose. The development of man is less a sequence of related individuals than a shifting of attention. And this keeps pace with the view of Time as dimension rather than flux, and of atoms as energies rather than minute but solid particles. The structure of the Universe may conceivably be better expressed in terms of related movements and efforts, than in terms of mass.

Such concepts are favourable to the flesh and spirit approach. They are also favourable to the Christian doctrine of Christ as representative man: the doctrine is most clearly expressed in Irenaeus, but it goes back through St. Paul and St. John to Christ Himself: it is scientifically less difficult to accept to-day than perhaps at any time in the last few centuries. The doctrine can only be expressed spatially: what if men are *actually* linked as the branches of a vine to its parent root? What if the fifteenth chapter of the fourth gospel be not parable but fact? An illustration of this, as related to conscious thought, was suggested to me by a book called *The Eternity of Time*, by Dr. A. P. Shepherd. We are like water lilies growing in a pond: the leaves and flowers are to all appearances separate, for the surface of the pond is the surface of consciousness: but we are in fact united to the root and to each other by stalks beneath the surface, which are seldom consciously perceived.[5]

If Jesus Christ is the final and personal Purpose of the Creator, then in Him all living creation is summed up (and here biology comes to our assistance, as far as animal life is concerned); His justification is our justification by something stronger than mere sentiment. Our existence is justified because through our fallen world perfection has been achieved in Jesus Christ. All honestly directed effort is redeemed and justified in Christ, however vacillating, however much mistaken. Only deliberately chosen falsehood remains unredeemed—for that is the sin against Holy Spirit—the denial that what is seen in Christ is indeed the mystery of godliness, manifested in flesh.

NOTES

[1] After reading this chapter, and especially the paragraphs about the Eucharist, my friend Mr. T. Westow (a member of the Roman Communion) said: 'Is not our trouble that under the influence of Greek thought the analysis took precedence over the whole, instead of our beginning with the whole and analyzing in conformity with the whole (in proportion and with perspective)?' I am sure he is right.

[2] In St. Luke 24: 37, we find an exception. Our Lord appeared to 'the eleven and those with them': they were terrified and 'supposed that they beheld a *pneuma*'. That this was, at least in Rome, considered to be a misuse of the word is indicated by the *Codex Bezae*, which has the reading '*phantasma*' instead of '*pneuma*', and by the quotation in Ignatius (Smyrn. III, 1), 'Take, feel me, and see that I am not a bodiless daemon'. Since Eusebius did not know the source of this quotation, and Origen and Jerome disagree as to its source—one said it was from the *Teaching of Peter*, and the other from the *Gospel according to the Hebrews*—we are entitled to suggest that Ignatius may have made the alteration himself, or that he knew the saying in Aramaic and translated better than St. Luke. The suggestion that the *Codex Bezae* has taken the word '*phantasma*' from the story of the walking on the sea in St. Mark may be true; but there is no sort of evidence that the word was substituted *by mistake*: and if it was done on purpose, it was presumably done for a reason which seemed good. Alternatively, we may believe that St. Luke himself originally wrote '*phantasma*', and that on revision he substituted the word '*pneuma*', which in popular use could mean 'ghost'. The spacing of letters in the *Codex Bezae* could also suggest a rather interesting translation of the reply of the Risen Lord, repunctuated thus: 'Feel me, and behold the spirit. Has it not got bones and flesh as you see that I have got?' In fact Jesus would be saying, 'Touch me and see what *the spirit* is. Not at all what you expected—not a *phantasma*—but with a solid body as you see that I have got.' The Christian idea of '*pneuma*' was new and strange, and it would not be impossible that it should have been toned down by successive scribes of a more liberal outlook. The Latin of the *Codex Bezae* does not support this reading: but neither does it support the clear reading '*to pneuma*'— its '*quoniam*' cannot have been the Greek '*to*', but '*hoti*'.

[3] *V.* Prof. G. W. H. Lampe, *The Seal of the Spirit*, pp. 113 f. and elsewhere. He would deny, however, any separation of the two sides of baptism, in the ritual and ceremonial of the second-century Church. I cannot wholly agree.

[4] The question of whether this reading was *Hōs*=who, or *Ho*=which, or *THEOS*=God, was once a great crux in the seventeenth and eighteenth

centuries. Our A.V. translates *Theos* from the *Textus Receptus*. *Hŏs* in Greek uncials is OΣ; *Theos* abbreviated is $\Theta\Sigma$; it is easy to see how one can have been mistaken for the other. *Hŏ* (=which) has much less authority. It is now fairly generally accepted that the right reading is *Hŏs*—who.

[5] It is ten years since I read Dr. Shepherd's book. The illustration I believe is mine, but the picture of conciousness as the surface of a pond comes from him. The water-lily on the dust-cover comes from my wife.

Chapter 8

CONQUEST

He was seen of angels: so that the angels too, with us, saw the Son of God, not seeing Him before (Chrys. P.G. 62, p. 554).

Not even they (the angels) saw the invisible nature of the Godhead, but when Incarnate they gazed at Him (Theodoret, comm. on 1 Tim. 3: 16).

When the Most High divided the nations, when He dispersed the sons of Adam, He fixed the boundaries of the nations according to the number of the angels of God. His people Jacob became the portion of the Lord, and Israel the measurement of His inheritance (Deut. 32: 8-9, Septuagint version).

JEWISH tradition held that: '. . . the destiny of the nations and of their heavenly princes is closely interwoven. God punishes no nation: nor will He, even in the time of the Messiah, punish any, until He shall have punished its guardian angel' (*Jewish Encycl.*, vol. I, art. 'Angelology').

There is no doubt that Jesus accepted and corroborated Jewish beliefs of His time. He certainly accepted and taught of a kingdom of evil set up against God (Matt. 9: 34 ff.). He accepted the devil's rights as prince of this world but not of any other (John 12: 31; 14: 30; 16: 11). His ministry and words shew that He recognized Himself as restricted in His mission to God's own people (until His resurrection): 'I am not sent, but unto the lost sheep of the house of Israel' (Matt. 15: 24); 'Go not into the way of the Gentiles . . .' (Matt. 10: 5).

The origins of Jewish angelology are irrelevant. Much may have come from Persia and Babylon, though even that has been disputed. What concerns us is, did Jesus accept it or not? If He did, then no matter what its origin, it is part of our Christian belief. If Persia and Babylon helped to turn Judaism into Christianity, it makes it no whit less Christian. Belief in guardian angels of nations interprets the national gods of polytheism

43

as fallen angels. 'We know that there are gods many and lords many,' said St. Paul, and we need not suppose that he spoke without authority: the early Church followed him in this, as we see in the fathers; these gods had some sort of personal (if infernal) reality. Those who deal with primitive tribes to-day are the slowest to deny some occult and personal power behind the objects of their cults. It is the long-distance observers—those who collate the material of the field anthropologist—who are most ready to explain away.

Our Lord's views on practical, historical or scientific affairs were not necessarily infallible. As man He had limited Himself to human knowledge. But in matters which come from what we call intuition or the sixth sense we cannot doubt Him. If we do, where shall we stop? His teaching and His Church's teaching is made up of things both new and old. The source of a doctrine taught by Him is interesting, but it is not always important. A most irritating person is the man who is always ready with 'I know where you got that from'—as if it affected the issue one way or the other. A belief is no less true because others have believed it before. The question is, what was the primitive teaching and what were its authorized developments?

First then, what inklings of the Jewish connexion of angels with nations can we find in the words and ministry of Christ?

'I am not sent but unto the lost sheep of the house of Israel,' was said to a Gentile woman who wished him to cast out a Gentile demon (Matt. 15: 21 ff.), an incident which is described in great detail.

This saying is a curious answer-which-was-no-answer to the disciples, who were already only too anxious to send her away. But she came and worshipped and made her request. The reply of Jesus shewed that He felt it His business to feed His own people first (if we look here at Mark 7: 27): the nations were at best 'hangers on' to the chosen people. She accepted the role of an outsider, and claimed His favour again—this time as a guest. They were in a house and possibly eating: she may well have suited her action to her words, and stooped down and picked up some crumbs and eaten them. She thereby made herself His guest, the 'stranger within their gates', who is to be treated as one of the chosen people. So the demon was cast out by virtue of the protection a host must give his guest. But though this was a foreshadowing of a ministry to Gentiles, it was done without the Messiah's trespassing beyond the limits of Israel, who was 'the portion of his inheritance'.

For the guardians of the nations were angels, and fallen angels. They had betrayed the commission granted them by God and had set themselves up as gods. This was the Jewish view and the view of the early Church (see espec. Justin Martyr, 1st Apol., 5). None the less, God would not punish any nation until He had punished its fallen guardian. Jesus would not cast out a foreign demon until He had won His victory; and we shall remember that the victory was the Cross. Not until after that was the Messiah free to go beyond the chosen people. Much evidence for this follows, and I must ask for patience.

But if we are to understand anything of the angelology both of the Jews and also of the early Church, we shall not look upon angels as single beings. The guardian angel of the nation was the archspirit in whom the spirits of men and women of that nation were vested. Like the archangels of Jacob Boehme, they embodied in themselves a host of lesser spirits, some incarnate in human beings, some mere wandering spirits seeking a human home. Those people 'possessed with unclean spirits' were those invaded by such wandering spirits.

Owing to the apostasy of the Jews, the 'gods' of the surrounding nations had been, as it were, invited within the borders of the chosen people. Many Jews were possessed with unclean spirits. These recognized Jesus, and the earliest healing in St. Mark is the casting out of one of these, who immediately sensed the hostile presence and cried out, 'What is between us and you? You came to destroy us. I know who you are, the Holy One of God' (Mark 1: 21 ff.).

It may be more than coincidence that the marginal reference from the verse which introduces this Markan passage is to St. Matthew 4: 13:

> Leaving Nazareth, he came and dwelt in Capernaum, which is by the sea, in the borders of Zebulun and Naphtali: that it might be fulfilled which was spoken by Isaiah the prophet, saying,

> The land of Zebulun and the land of Naphtali,
> The way of the sea, beyond Jordan,
> Galilee of the nations,
> The people which sat in darkness
>   Saw a great light,
> And to them which sat in the region and
> Shadow of death
>   To them did light spring up.

In Galilee of the nations the light began to shine, and the first who saw it was a trespassing spirit.

A later confession of the same kind came from a man possessed of an unclean spirit which was a battalion of spirits in itself (Mark 5: 1–20). St. Matthew adds to the Markan version (Matt. 8: 29) the spirit's reproach of Jesus for coming to torment it 'before the time'. Before what time? The time, presumably, when Jesus should have earned the right by conquest. St. Luke adds that the spirit demanded not to be sent 'into the abyss' (Luke 8: 31), but into the herd of swine that was feeding on the hillside—which in itself is a sign that the people were not strict Jews.

Strangely, it may seem to us, and with some significance at which we can only guess, Jesus respected this claim. In some sense the spirit had a right to be there—it was a foreign devil. Accordingly the Messiah did not 'punish' it, but allowed it to destroy itself.

The Septuagint quotation from Deuteronomy which heads this chapter (which is repeatedly quoted in the fathers) is the myth of the divine commission to the angel guardians. They misused their commission (*vide infra*) and became fallen angels, and thus the divine array which linked heaven and earth was broken. The number of the angels and nations was the recurrent seventy (or seventy-two—the difference is not important and recurs in the variant readings wherever the significant seventy occurs, whether in the Old or New Testaments). Has Jesus left us anything to suggest His acceptance of that myth?

One thinks at once of the Lukan account of the mission of the seventy, and then perhaps it seems after all to have no connexion.

When the seventy returned from their mission and announced with triumphant delight: 'Lord, even the demons are subject to us in Thy Name'; Jesus replied: 'I beheld Satan fallen as lightning from heaven.' Satan was prince of this world, and his commission extended over the kingdoms of this world *and their glory*: this, his claim in the Temptations, was not denied. But in this mission of His Church, Jesus saw Satan's tyranny at an end. But He pointed out even greater reason for joy, their own (seventy) names were written in heaven. We shall return to this.

St. Luke makes it quite clear that he is not confusing two incidents. 'In that very hour', he says, 'he rejoiced in the Holy Spirit, and said, I thank Thee, O Father, Lord of heaven and earth, that thou didst hide these things from the wise and understanding, and didst reveal them unto babes: yea, Father; for so it was well-pleasing in Thy sight' (Luke 10: 17-21).

With all this apparatus and emphasis, it is surely inconceivable that the mission of the seventy should be another account of the mission of the twelve, with disagreement in numbers. St. Luke only repeats his accounts deliberately and for a reason. He could only have made a mistake here if he got from two sources two accounts of the mission of the twelve, one with numbers much exaggerated. He was an intelligent man and would have his eyes open to the possibility of there being two stories of the same mission. To suggest that he gladly and uncritically accepted the account of the seventy as foreshadowing the preaching to Gentiles is to misunderstand St. Luke. He was remarkably faithful to his sources, as we know from his use of St. Mark. And if he had wanted and was unscrupulous enough to use this story as Gentile propaganda, why did he not suggest that the Gentiles were included in the tour?

The charge given to the seventy by Jesus was not in all ways like that given to the twelve. It is quite like it as reported by St. Matthew: but if we compare the charge to the seventy with the charge to the twelve in St. Luke, there are important differences. St. Matthew may well have fused the two, as he often did.

In St. Luke, however, the twelve were to be sowers of the word; they were to preach and heal: the seventy were to reap the harvest which the twelve had sown; they were only to announce the nearness of the Kingdom to such cities as received them, and there to heal their sick. Tyre and Sidon would be better off than the cities which had rejected him, and Sodom better off than such as rejected them. The mission of the seventy offered the chosen people their final choice: it was not yet a mission to the Gentiles, but it foreshadowed it. Their triumph over the demons was pronounced by Christ to be the fall of Satan and of the powers subject to him. There is little doubt that the saying is authentic.[1]

Here again then we find Jesus Himself thinking and acting within the pattern of Jewish angelology. God had created seventy nations to fit seventy angels (or seventy-two). The angels had abused their commission and failed in God's purpose for them, as the twelve chosen tribes had also failed. The mission of the Messiah was therefore a double one: first to reconstitute the twelve tribes, in the twelve apostles: and second to re-create the divine pattern of the nations in the mission of the seventy. The result of the mission was to re-establish a spiritual ascendancy (to regain the initiative, in the jargon of to-day), and to write seventy new names in heaven to take the place of the fallen guardians.

In this way the broken array was mended (Appendix). When the powers of heaven were shaken from their places, which they no longer deserved, there were other names to take those places: the sign of it was the subjection of the spirits to them. In the same way there were twelve new tribes ready in the new Israel. The divine pattern was regained, and the divine purpose for creation restored.

It is difficult to rid our minds of the feeling that thought patterns of this kind are childish and unimportant. 'Surely Jesus Himself conformed to the patterns of those among whom He lived? If He did think in those patterns, have they any real relevance to-day? Did not His acceptance of such patterns belong to His self-limitation as Son of Man?' But did He conform to the patterns of those among whom He lived? His attitude to the Sabbath was not conformity; yet that was the very centre of the worship of the Pharisees. He did not conform to the traditions which had become valueless—tithes, ceremonial impurity, scribal exposition of the Torah, the exclusiveness of Temple worship. In these things He was the 'new wine' and did not hesitate to say so. But the thought patterns which He learnt from Judaism and retained, He retained because they were valuable.

The number seventy[2] had much meaning for Jews. Seventy angels, seventy nations, seventy elders, seventy members of the Sanhedrin: they were part of the pattern and form of the divine myth. Jesus accepted and used it in the mission of the seventy. We are not to literalize and say that our Lord by the sending out of the seventy laid it down that there are seventy nations in the realm of ideas with seventy guardian angels, who fell from grace and needed replacement. But there is a significance in numbers, though our pattern of thought to-day pretends not to recognize it. The chief significance, scientifically and sacramentally, is that numbers make us able to see associations between ideas which we might otherwise not have noticed.

The truth which our Lord's choice of seventy conveys is that nations are God-given: their differences are more than skin deep, and have an eternal purpose in heaven as on earth: war and disorder among them are not part of the divine plan. But the breaking down of barriers between nations, which Paul speaks of, does not mean the end of God's purpose for them as nations, but the end of exclusiveness.

In the epistles of St. Paul it is difficult to see exactly where to place the principalities and powers. Were they powers of evil, or something between good and evil? They were, he said, the archons of this age (1 Cor. 2: 8): if they were the fallen angels of the nations, and if they confessed Jesus as Christ through their servants the unclean spirits, it cannot be supposed that they did not recognize Jesus, or that they 'crucified the Lord of glory' in ignorance of His identity as some of the Fathers seem to suggest.

What Paul does suggest is that they did not understand God's plan for the Christ. They knew Him and feared Him and crucified Him, but *they did not know what they were doing*: the first word from the cross may be held to refer to them as much as to their human agents: they, like men, were conquered by forgiveness. The whole thing was God's plan, His 'wisdom in mystery, which had been kept secret, which God foreordained before the ages for our glory'—but the whole passage (1 Cor. 2) should be read with this in mind, if possible in Greek, and the parable of the husbandmen should be read immediately afterwards (Mark 12: 1–12).

No doubt St. Mark is right in saying that 'the chief priests and scribes and elders', who had challenged the authority of Jesus, took the parable as directed against themselves: and so in a sense it was: but it was not the custom of Jesus to waste parables by using them simply as weapons against his opponents. In fact the parable contains the answer to the question which they had just asked Him, and which He had refused to give in so many words, 'In what authority are you doing this, and who gave you authority to do it?' 'That I will not tell you, but I will tell you a story'—which they promptly applied to themselves, but which had also a profounder significance. The vineyard had produced wild grapes: if Jesus was thinking back to Isaiah, Chapter 5, the sad song of the vineyard, He would be thinking in terms of verse 7 of it: '. . . the vineyard of the Lord of hosts is the house of Israel, and the men of Judah His pleasant plant.' The vineyard and the vine represent the chosen people, and the husbandmen are those who have made it what it is, who killed the heir that the inheritance might be theirs, who crucified the Lord of glory: they were the 'archons of this age'—the 'principalities and powers in heavenly places', who stood between man and God. Those same powers, Paul gives us to understand, were reconciled to Christ by that same death, and through Him to God (Col. 1: 20). No small scale or purely human atonement is enough for St. Paul: it is the whole creation which is reconciled, as Ignatius and Irenaeus testified, in heaven and earth and under the earth. We get a glimpse of a God who recognized a sort of primordial right in His creatures to claim His life from Him. Through the submission of the Guardians of the nations, He Himself in Christ regained access to those same nations: in 'the dispensation of the unsearchable riches of Christ' to the nations, God is justified afresh before their Guardians, from whom the mystery had been hidden (Eph. 3: 1–12).

To those who suppose that 'the mystery hidden from the ages' was simply the admission of Gentile converts without circumcision, it must sometimes have seemed that Paul made rather heavy weather with his mystery; '*parturiunt montes, nasce-*

tur . . .' not a 'ridiculus mus', but at least a much smaller child than was expected. If we see that the very powers of heaven are reconciled by the conversion of the Gentiles (Eph. 3: 1–12), we shall begin to understand St. Paul's language. If we go on to realize that this was rooted in the teaching of Jesus Christ Himself, we may also begin to understand an Atonement in which we are sharers with angels and ghosts, 'energies' of Nature and the host of heaven.

And when the cosmic Guardians have been reconciled, what then? There remains the unholy brood which they have let loose, still gathered under an unrepentant antagonist who has not been reconciled. The fathers should be read on this subject, especially Tertullian and Justin Martyr and Lactantius (Appendix, sec. C). Satan is fallen from heaven; the dragon has come down to earth, and with the help of the unruly passions left behind by the fallen powers he has set up his kingdom in opposition to God on the last battlefield which remains to him.

For Satan is other than a fallen angel. He is the first principle of evil and the cause of the angelic fall. Causally he comes before the fall of the angels, for such things cannot be spoken of in terms of time. Satan objectifies in himself the potential evil inherent in spirit, which is freedom. The fall of the angels was not the first pre-cosmic fall (see Appendix); Paul at least hints at that, and the idea is expanded in later patristic thought.[3]

This is the language of myth, through which alone spiritual truth can be spoken. The first danger is that the language of myth should be taken literally. Are we not, then, to take it seriously? All mythological truth is to be taken seriously, but not literally. It tells what has happened, but it is myth not history—not even legend; but what it tells is truth, and deeper truth than can be told in a pedestrian record of events. The second danger therefore is of thinking that myth is not true at all. If myth is not history, neither is it fantasy. Myth and history meet only at one central point, in Christ the Mystery who embodies both. Bearing this in mind, we can safely return to the Christian myth of the angelic fall, and of the reconciliation of the angels in Jesus Christ.

In his commentary on 1 Peter, Dr. Selwyn has suggested that the sense of the second verb in Chapter III, verse 19 (*ĕkēruxĕn*) is 'proclaimed' rather than 'preached' (pp. 197–201 and Essay I, pp. 314–62). I am sure he is right. But when he says that the proclamation was made 'to the disobedient angels who could not, in the ordinary sense of the term, repent, but who could be brought into subjection', he misses the point of Colossians 1: 19–21, combined with Philippians 2: 9–11, combined with Ephesians 3: 10–11.

These passages shew a process of atonement in three stages: (1) conquest of the guardian Powers by Christ, and their submission; (2) free access to the nations on earth, by virtue of the submission of their Guardians; the Church preaches a missionary gospel; (3) the making known to the Guardians *through their own nations* of the 'manifold wisdom of God', in which they are reconciled.

The thought of an angelic redemption underlies much of St. Paul's teaching about the Powers. And it is theologically and philosophically essential that we should recognize the Atonement as the triumph of persuasion over force, not only on earth but in the realm of the spirit also.

The reconciliation of fallen spirits restored proper order in creation: 'kosmos' returned. Fallen spirits, says Tatian, are like letters in a manuscript: their activities are meaningless in isolation, but convey a real meaning in their proper order (adv. Graec. XVII). The angelic array has been broken: and Papias says:

> To some of them (clearly the angels which at first were holy) He gave dominion also over the arrangement of the Universe, and He commissioned them to exercise their dominion well; (and he says next) but it so befel that their array came to nought; for the great dragon, the old serpent, who is also called Satan and the devil, was cast down, yea and was cast down to the earth, he and his angels. [4]

The array was broken, and the commissioned guardians thrown into disorder: a restored order among them had to precede restored order on earth, or at least must be an accompaniment of it.

It is difficult for the twentieth century to see that angelic orders and hierarchies can have any central importance in a confession of faith, or indeed anywhere else. That is because we expect to find a true and final meaning in history. But the Christian only finds true and final meaning in a Christ who left the plane of history. His exodus from history (in the human sense) was the beginning of true meaning. The Apostles' creed does not end with the words 'suffered under Pontius Pilate, was crucified, dead, and buried'. Yet, with those words it does in fact leave historical sequence, and returns on the third day which is beyond ordinary history. Unless we realize that, we shall make neither sense nor meaning of Easter, Ascension-tide and Whitsun. The witnesses of the Resurrection were witnesses of ultra-historical truth, or they were nothing. 'If in this life only we have hope in Christ, we are of all men most miserable'—for our curtain will fall on tragedy, which is no more than the highest human solution: it is no answer to despair.

The reconstitution of the angelic orders, and the conquest of the hierarchy of evil, were and are essentials of the Christian faith. They belong to the confession of Jesus as Christ, Son, and Lord (O. Cullmann, *Earliest Christian Confessions*, pp. 57–64).

Sources of later post-Apostolic doctrines may be genuinely important to shew the authorized developments of these doctrines. What is added to the *kerygma* must be checked and counter-checked. But belief in guardian angels of the nations is an integral part of the doctrine of the atonement.

Professor Cullmann writes:

The formula of 1 Tim. 3: 16, alludes to the angelic powers: 'seen of angels' [—and a footnote at this point adds]: 'The continuation, "preached unto the Gentiles", alludes probably to Christ's preaching to the dead. This preaching is thus mentioned before the Ascension. The descent into hell is brought into connection on the one hand with the preaching to the dead (1 Peter 3: 18 f.), and on the other with the conquest of the powers of Hades. . . .

The one (i.e. the confession) cited in the *Epistle of Polycarp* (Chap. II, 1) does not forget to add, after mentioning the resurrection, that the 'glory and throne at God's right hand are assigned to Christ', and that to Him 'all heavenly and earthly beings are subject, and everything which breathes serves Him'. . . . The more matured confession of Ignatius of Antioch (Trall. IX, 1) clearly exhibits the regularity with which the *epourania*, the *epigeia*, and the *hupochthonia* appear in the oldest symbols: '. . . he was crucified and died, the beings in heaven and earth and under the earth saw him'. . . . Ignatius put the Christological formula transmitted to him at the service of his polemic against the Docetists. Hence he here makes the powers *witnesses* of the reality of the death and bodily resurrection of Christ. But it is apparent that originally here, as in the earlier confessions, the only thing that matters is their subjection. The fact that Ignatius retained mention of these powers, while assigning them a new role, confirms that we are dealing here with a *constant and central* element in all confessions of the first century (*Earliest Christian Confessions*, pp. 60–1).

I agree with almost all that Professor Cullmann has said. But there is, I believe, more importance to be attached to the *witness* of the death and resurrection by angels than he attaches to it. The most important thing is certainly their subjection. The proclamation to the spirits in prison' (the fallen angels) is a summons to witness: it is because they witness that they submit: the departed of the nations see their submission, which opens the prison doors for them.

'Having put off from himself his body, he made a show of the principalities and the powers openly, triumphing over them in it' (the cross) (Col. 2: 15).

This note of triumph over the powers of evil, whether infernal or heavenly, persists in creeds and credal formulae throughout the patristic age, and is still found in the creed of St. Patrick (N. J. D. White, *Hist. of Church of Ireland*; ed. W. A. Phillips, i, 105).

NOTES

[1] Dr. T. W. Manson supports this: *Sayings of Jesus*, p. 258.

[2] The number 70 may suggest new associations of ideas. If the true readings be 70 and not 72, we shall see in it a combination of divine and human —the divine number in creation multiplied by the human count of ten—the flesh and spirit principle expressed in mathematical terms. The fathers support 70 in their quotation of Ex. 15: 27, and Num. 33: 9. See Tert. adv. Marc., IV, 24; Orig. Hom. 7 in Exod.; Hom. 27 in Num.; Jerome, Ep. 69: 6.

On the alternative 72, see Plummer, I.C.C., *St. Luke*, ad loc; the weight of evidence is for 70. But 72 need not lack numerical significance, being a combination of the divinely chosen 12 (tribes) multiplied by the purely human 6—the 'number of a man'. The Threefold 6 was the 'number of the beast' (man without God), the infernal trinity, the thrice repeated blasphemy of the week without the sabbath, the threefold defiance of God. It is interesting to find in some purely pagan countries the week without the sabbath— the 6-day week—still surviving against Christian and Moslem influence: e.g. in the Northern Territories of the Gold Coast.

[3] This is clear in 1 Enoch, Ch. LXIX. See also E. Langton, *Essentials of Demonology*, pp. 113 f.; Origen, de Prin. Bk. I, Chs. I and V; Lactantius, Inst. II, 9. Also *v.* Appendix.

[4] Andr. Caes. quoting Papias; Lightfoot, App. Frs, p. 521. For an alternative view cf. Novatian, de Trin. 18, 19, 20. See also Orig. c. Cels. I, 68. Psellus, *de operatione daemonum.*

E

Chapter 9

ARCHETYPES, ANGELS AND BEASTS

IDOLATRY, says the Didache, is the worship of dead gods. And the teaching of the Ante-Nicene Fathers is summed up in Athanasius, who made it clear that *death* and *non-existence* meant for the Church a *condition leading to death.* Jesus said little, even indirectly, about idolatry: His preaching was to the people of Israel who were 'the Lord's portion', so that He had no occasion for discourses on idolatry in the ordinary sense. None the less the mission of the seventy shewed that He accepted the belief of His time in angel guardians of the nations (Ch. 15, *infra*). It is easier to believe that He did so, because He clearly stated his belief in angel guardians of individuals (Matt. 18: 10). He also shewed in the story of the demoniac named Legion, a curious respect for the territorial rights of those demons; He did not banish them but let them banish themselves.

I have said that the Jewish belief in angel guardians of the nations was a monotheistic interpretation of the beliefs of those nations themselves in tribal and national gods: it was the insight of an inspired people into the claims of idolatry (1 Cor. 8). The gods of the nations were not imaginary in the sense of having no sort of existence in time; but their authority as gods was unreal. They existed but not for worship.

Primitive religion to-day gropes towards this same realization. I will speak only of tribes of which I have had personal experience and into whose language, customs and religion I have made research locally.

Northern Togoland is occupied by a number of tribes known generally as 'Konkomba', or more properly Kpunkpamba. Most of these have settled within traditional memory where they now are: but there is a substratum of 'people of the land'. After their settlement came the invasion of the present ruling Dagbamba, with a loosely knit constitution of Chiefs, Elder-

56

chiefs, and Heir-chiefs. There are therefore three main strata: originals, immigrants, and invaders.

Their religious and archetypal ideas are embodied in their mythology, which is distinct from tribal legends. Here, for instance is a myth of creation and fall, which provides an explanation of how local and tribal gods came to exist.

In the old dark days, Nawuni (God) created man and set him to live on a rocky plain, full of holes, chasms and abysses. The surface was so slippery and the chasms were so horrible that men dared not move at all. They prayed to Nawuni, who then created sand, gravel and clay, which he ordered his messengers to spread abroad over the earth. This they did, but with a high angelic carelessness, which accounts for the number of rocky hills still projecting above the surface.

Man, now able to walk where he would, became proud and ceased to care for Nawuni and his worship. So Nawuni thought out a scheme for enforcing the allegiance of men and angels. He called them to him, and shewed them a wonderful and new thing which he had created, the belly, for before that men had had no bellies.

Men were foolishly delighted with these, especially when Nawuni explained the pleasure which they brought with them, the solid joy of eating and the wild exhilaration of drink. So men prayed Nawuni to give them bellies, which Nawuni gladly did. (This is a good example of the law of prayer: for good or ill, men are only given what they pray for.) Thus men became dependent upon Nawuni for their daily bread.

The angels were wiser and refused to pray for these gifts; so they preserved their independence, and were given positions of rule and authority in the earth. They became the *tingbana* (perhaps the 'skins of earth'), each with his or her own territory on earth of which the rights, fertility and power belonged to them.

The story goes on to describe the coming of death, caused by the seduction of man's messenger, the dog, by an evil Djinnee. The dog was carrying man's prayer for Life to Nawuni, but was delayed by the Djinnee; meanwhile the malignant goat reached Nawuni with a false message that man chose Death. So Death was decreed as the lot of man.[1]

Here we have a primitive account of the fall of man, through

desire for transient pleasure. We also have an account of the
establishment of guardians over areas of the earth. The implications of this simple creation myth are to be seen clearly in the
ritual and ceremonial of the 'people of the land'—that is, of
such tribes as claim to be aboriginal. [2] Amongst them there is no
divorce between ancestor worship and the tendance of the local
guardian of the land, the tingbane. The spirits of the departed
are taken into the spirit hierarchy of the tribe which is also
guardian of the tribal territory. Worship is of the 'do ut des'
type: there is peace on earth, at least within their boundaries.

In most areas the people of the land have been overrun but
not destroyed. They have continued their tendance of the shrine
but the secular power belongs to their conquerors. The conquering tribe lives in a continual tension between its own guardian spirit into which its own departed are taken at death, and
the guardian of the land who is hostile to invaders and has to be
propitiated. The conquering tribe is safe so long as it is on good
terms with the priestly family of the land.

But invaders from elsewhere, however long ago, have their
own shrines to tend: these are often far away in pool, grove or
mountain where according to tribal history they first became a
tribe. Thus the soul of the Ya-Na, Chief of the Dagbamba, is at
his death led by phantom drummers through the bush to the
pool of Bagale-biung, to enter the sacred lake in the form of a
hippopotamus, where he remains to await reincarnation in one
of his own descendants in due course. That is his spiritual home.
His real authority is as king over his own people, and ultimately
(though he will deny this) not over the land in which his people
live—or only by consent of the priests of the local shrines. On
their land he is still a religious trespasser, allowed to remain on
sufferance, so long as he pays his due sacrifices to the divinely
commissioned guardians.

In other areas the priestly families were exterminated, and
the local shrines are now tended by substitutes. In some at least
of such instances the guardian of the land is propitiated rather
than tended, with a sullen and unhappy ceremonial of aversion.
Such guardian spirits become 'angels of punishment'. They are
powerful, and useful for invocations and oaths. They have lost
their link with earth and have no animal form to symbolize

them, but are spirits of lightning, wind and storm: their shrines are rocks or caves or mountains.

But those spirits who are still true guardians have for the most part forms of beasts of one kind or another. This is not the place to discuss totem and tabu. But there is an archetypal validity about these forms in which the guardians are given shape. They are paralleled in the Old Testament not only in the calf of Baal (Hos. 8: 6) and the 'hairy ones' or he-goats,[3] and the animal forms of many of the gods of the nations (Ezek. 8: 10; Baruch 3: 16), but also in much of the symbolism of the prophetic visions (Zeph. 7: 14). The beast forms of angels and demons are particularly significant (Ezek. 1: 5, 10; 10: 14; Num. 21: 6-8). In Isaiah (5: 29 f.) the spirits of the nations are heard roaring as lions, who lay hold of Israel their prey (cf. also Nah. 2: 11 f.; Isa. 30: 6). In Jeremiah (8: 17) they are pictured as serpents and basilisks (cf. also Deut. 8: 15; Isa. 14: 29) which will not be charmed. But in the reconciliation of the Messianic king the dominion of man over the beasts will be re-established (Isa. 11: 1-9; Mic. 7: 17) as the outward sacramental sign of renewed dominion of the chosen people over the rebellious spirits of the nations—the fallen angels.[4] 'God in Christ redeemed man, Man in Christ redeemed nature'—that is the sacrament to which the prophets looked forward, and which was fulfilled in Jesus Christ the Mystery.

The intuitive concept of tribal and national guardians as theriomorphic, which is common to primitive religious intuition and prophetic vision, is seen again in the pictures and visions of the fallen kingdom of Satan, in the early centuries of the history of the Church. Christian hermits were assailed by demons in animal forms (Athan., Vita S. Ant., ed. J. Annison, Paris 1698, p. 813, A, B, vol. III): in medieval sculptures lost souls are herded to perdition by devils with animal heads and talons.

These are images, as the figures of prophetic vision were images: but the question remains whether such images are valid for all time or refer only to the time and environment of the visionary. The psychology of Dr. Jung suggests that there is something constant in the images themselves, which are archetypal and have something eternally true about them. So Dr.

Layard (a follower of Dr. Jung), in *The Lady of the Hare*, finds a persistently recurrent image in the hare:

> . . . the hare was to be numbered among what Jung calls the 'Archetypes', by which is meant symbolic images pregnant with power that have had great influence in the past and which live on in the deeper levels of the unconscious of Modern Man, unknown to and therefore inoperative in most, but ready to spring forth into effective action once the internal redemptive process is activated and begins to work (p. 25).

Charles Williams has developed this idea in *The Place of the Lion*, with considerable effect.

But unless we can find sanction for this archetypal parallelism between angels, beasts and spirits of nations, in the New Testament itself, we shall still as Christians be at sea. Is the subjection of angels a sacramental parallel to the dominion of man over the beasts? Are those Old Testament images reborn within the Christian Church? Or are they part of the apparatus which Christ and His Church shed—something which belongs to primitive religion but not to its full development in Christianity?

In spite of Dr. Farrer, the Revelation of St. John is still suspect. But he has laid down a principal which is fundamental:

> Christ in his earthly life had made the decisive transformation of the images, and he had given his Spirit to continue the work in the minds of the disciples, to lead them into the knowledge of all the truth (*Rebirth of Images*, p. 16).

We do in fact find beast images of angels, and beast forms of fallen angels who lead nations astray. But even so it is difficult to feel that these reborn images give the full Christian authentication that we need. We want something nearer home, an authentication in the preaching of the apostles, or if possible even something from Christ Himself.

Nor need we fail to find it. A glance at the word *thērion* (wild beast) in Moulton and Geden's Greek Testament Concordance takes us first to St. Mark's brief account of the Temptations of our Lord. There we see three stages of temptation, as in the other Synoptists, but at first sight three different stages. Jesus was in the wilderness forty days being tempted by Satan: He was with the wild beasts: angels ministered to Him. Our first feeling may be of surprise, at the sandwiching of wild beasts between two sets of spiritual powers, Satan and ministering angels. How inconsequent of St. Mark!—according to what was until lately an accepted view, how like St. Mark! Just what Papias suggested (Euseb. H.E. III, 39), quoting 'the Elder'; St. Mark did not write 'in order'. But 'the Elder', or Papias, also said something else: 'Mark made no mistake, while he thus wrote down some things as he remembered them; for he made it his one care not to omit anything that he heard, or to set down any false statement therein.' He also calls St. Mark 'the interpreter of Peter'.

If we accept what Papias has said, we do not necessarily expect historical order in St. Mark. But surely St. Mark brought the wild beasts into a spiritual experience for a good reason? Or is it no more than one of those vivid 'eye-witness' touches which we have come to expect in his stories? But neither St. Mark nor St. Peter was eye-witness of the Temptations. And the arrangement here is something more than a failure in historical order. Whatever St. Mark's historical order (and we think better of it than we used to do) he was not inconsequent in thought; and if he seems so to us, Dr. Lightfoot and Dr. Farrer have done much to show that the fault lies in our own thinking more than in his. An older generation of Christian thought which, like the New Testament writers, was soaked in the Old Testament and its sequences of ideas, was less inclined to find the New Testament inconsequent.

Psalm 91 gives a picture of the man who 'dwells in the secret place of the Most High'. He passes through demons of the night and day,[5] but is kept safe by the ministry of angels. With their support he treads upon dangerous wild beasts, lions and snakes; but just as the four demons of the waste, in verses 5 and 6, are named after their visible effects—terror, sunstroke, pestilence, fever—so probably these wild beasts are images of something more than ordinary lions and snakes. With that Psalm in mind, perhaps, St. Mark was not so inconsequent. Satan, demons, angels—if the 'wild beasts' are demons—have at least a clearly seen connexion. But there still seems something illogical in the order. Jesus first met the Prince of demons and was tempted: then (St. Mark observes) he was with demons. But surely that needs no saying? Satan does not go unattended. Why Satan first, and then the demons?

We have seen above that not only demons but the fallen angels of the nations are pictured theriomorphically in various parts of the Old Testament (Appendix, sec. B). The contemporary interpretation appears in the Ethiopic Enoch.[6] The Watchers or Guardians were condemned and sentenced to imprisonment 'for their unrighteousness in becoming subject to Satan, and leading astray those who dwell on the earth' (LIV, 6): these remained in perpetual darkness. But their spiritual progeny, the demons, remained free 'to work moral ruin on the earth without hindrance till the final judgment' (Introd., p. cv): they are the hosts of Satan.

It would be difficult to find a more effective symbolism to describe the psychology of unconscious mind. The archetypal ideas fallen and distorted lie buried in the profound darkness of the abyss of unconscious mind. But their misbegotten brood of fears, complexes and inhibitions remains free to work moral ruin on the earth. They find expression in the forms which belong to myths or dreams—for myths are no more than the community dream. Many of these forms are beast forms, which readily lend themselves to the expression of a single archetype. Man's failure to control the beasts buried in his own unconscious is sacramentally expressed in his loss of dominion over the animal world.

Assume for a moment that St. Mark was using the word 'wild beast' symbolically. At least his order has become logical. Jesus was first tempted by the evil principle in his most obvious form. He then reached less accessible ground, and found Himself among the wild beasts, who are the perversions of archetypal ideas, isolated and therefore unbalanced, demonic. Through them He reached the very fallen Powers themselves—fallen, but not beyond redemption. Still unshaken, the Christ received their submission: in Him they were conquered and redeemed, and their order restored. Their demonic nature disappeared in the renewal of their balance. As angels again, they ministered to Him. *But even their ministry was part of His temptation.* For the temptation of man unfallen, or man restored, is to accept angelic ministry and use it for purposes which are demonic—in fact to tempt the Lord His God.

More must be said about this, but not until we have more fully linked up the theriomorphic archetypes with the nations, in the New Testament as well as in the Old. Primitive religion agrees with the Old Testament in connecting the two, but Christian sanction is also needed.

The next reference in the Greek Testament Concordance under *thērion* is to St. Peter's own account of his vision at Joppa (Acts 11: 6). In it he told the Jerusalem Church that he saw wild beasts whom he regarded as unclean, but was told by God that God Himself had made them clean: he then went under the guidance of the Holy Ghost and preached to a Gentile congregation, and so released upon them the same Holy Ghost of whom he was possessed. Hearing Peter's account, the apostles and brethren at once glorified God, and said: 'Then to the nations also has God given repentance unto life.' There is no sort of doubt here that the wild beasts were the spirits of the nations: we can see that, but what is so impressive is that the Jerusalem Church at once saw it, too. Perhaps in St. Mark's account of the Temptations the word *thēria* (wild beasts) was Peter's word: they were the same wild beasts with whom the tempted Christ kept company. But whether it was Peter's word as interpreting the experience, or not, there can be no doubt that the account of the experience came from Christ Himself.

Peter is not alone, in the New Testament, in his vision of archetypal beasts. St. Paul referred to a time when 'after the manner of men he fought with wild beasts at Ephesus' (1 Cor. 15: 32). This follows a perplexing passage about 'baptism for the dead', which in its turn follows a passage about the subjection of all 'rule and authority and power' to Christ. Whatever baptism for the dead may mean, there is no doubt what the subjection of all things to Christ meant in Paul's language. It was the conquest of the world rulers of this darkness, the principalities and the powers, who had rebelled. Commentators have remarked on the abrupt transition; but having in mind the symbolism of the beasts we may find it less abrupt. Paul is most unlikely to have been put into the arena: he was a Roman citizen—and anyhow there is no other reference to such a thing.

What we do know about his stay at Ephesus is that there were there not only exorcists and possessed persons, but also many who practised 'curious arts', who were won over by Paul, and who burnt their books (Acts 19: 19). The practice of curious arts usually consists in binding 'the Powers' with spells, and then making use of them for good or evil purposes.

If Paul, together with the early Church, knew 'the Powers' under the forms of wild beasts, then the word *ethēriomachēsa* was a natural enough word to use for his battle with their possessors. He had fought 'after the manner of men', he 'stood in jeopardy every hour': his 'wrestling was not against flesh and blood, but against the principalities, against the powers, against the world-rulers of this darkness, against the spiritual hosts of wickedness in the heavenly places'. But the risk which he ran was profitless 'if the dead be not raised': and perhaps 'being baptized for the dead' may have something to do with the early Church's claim that no spell or necromancy could succeed if a baptized Christian were present.

We may now return to the other Synoptic accounts of the Temptation, and see how the Markan account fits them, in the light of this interpretation of the wild beasts. It will be assumed that the order in Luke is the original Q order (if in despite of Dom B. C. Butler and Dr. Farrer we can still believe in Q). Dr. Manson has pointed out in *The Sayings of Jesus* (p. 43) that St. Matthew's account works up to a grand artistic climax, and St. Luke would not have altered it if his information supported that order. This seems a good reason for preferring St. Luke's order. St. Mark's account of the Temptation must have come from Jesus Himself, perhaps through Peter. Is it not possible that the accounts in St. Matthew and St. Luke (whether through Q or not) were by way of being interpretations of the original account in St. Mark? The interpretation may have come from our Lord Himself: I personally think it most likely that it did (I find it difficult to be patient with those who assume that all interpretations of parables were added later by the evangelists, or by the *kerygma* of the early Church). The saying 'To you it has been given to know the mystery of the Kingdom of God: but to those outside all things are done in parables' has

good authority, though it offends some who think that it is not
the sort of thing that Jesus would have said. We can only judge
what sort of things Jesus would have said by the things which
our evidence tells us He did in fact say; and there is no textual
evidence against this saying. Such a saying would lose its meaning unless Jesus had interpreted to His disciples much that was
not publicly interpreted. It is at least possible that, in the account of the Temptation in St. Luke, Jesus Himself interpreted
His own brief account which we have in St. Mark. Does it make
sense as an interpretation of it?

Jesus was baptized and was 'driven' or 'led' by the Spirit into
the wilderness, as Israel was both driven and led into the wilderness after baptism in the Red Sea (1 Cor. 10: 2). There he remained forty days, as Israel had remained forty years. He was,
says St. Mark, being tempted by Satan: St. Luke follows this,
but alters 'Satan' to 'the devil' and adds that He ate nothing and
became hungry; He was tempted to turn stones into bread. This
takes us straight back to Deuteronomy (8: 3):[7] '. . . and he
humbled thee, and suffered thee to hunger, and fed thee with
manna, which thou knewest not, neither did thy fathers know;
that he might make thee know that man doth not live by bread
only, but by every thing that proceedeth out of the mouth of the
Lord doth man live.' Israel was God's son and was tempted in
the wilderness: here again Israel was tempted in the person of
Jesus, who had been proclaimed as God's Son in His baptism.
The first temptation in St. Luke and St. Matthew interprets St.
Mark's brief statement that Jesus was in the wilderness forty
days tempted of Satan. He was tempted by His hunger; He was
tempted to doubt His Sonship and to try out His powers quietly
by Himself; He was tempted to become the popular kind of
social reformer who would satisfy the poor with bread.

'He was hungry,' says St. Luke. Later on, too, St. Luke tells
us that Peter was hungry, and in his hunger saw a vision. Here,
I think, St. Luke wishes us to understand that after the forty
days Jesus, too, saw a vision. Not, be it said, a dream, or a
purely subjective experience: fasting is often the gateway to the
sight of truth. When *we* fast, our visions are of the jumbled type
that our fallen nature produces—a mixture of truth and delu-
sion. When Jesus fasted, His vision was not vitiated, but shewed

Him a world which is normally hidden. The devil 'led Him up': here is no mention of a high mountain, for this was an ascent in a new dimension; Jesus found Himself on a point of time from which all the kingdoms of the world were visible; He was on the plane where the very spirits of the nations were gathered. 'These', said Satan, 'have been given to me on the plane of authority committed to me; I commit them to whom I please of those who serve me. Submit and worship, as these spirits have submitted, and I will give all this authority and glory to you.'

Peter also saw the nations of the world as 'quadrupeds of the earth and wild beasts and creeping things and the birds of the heaven,' enclosed in 'a certain vessel' ('*skeuos ti*', Acts 11: 5 f.).

Two chapters earlier (9: 15) Ananias had been told that Saul was to be a 'vessel of choice' (*skeuos eklogēs*), a 'repository of the power of Jesus' (*v.* Souter, under '*skeuos*'), and Paul had no doubt that the good pleasure of God for him was 'to reveal his Son in me, that I might preach him among the Gentiles'. As a result of this Paul 'conferred not with flesh and blood': he did not go to Jerusalem to those which were apostles before him, but to Arabia and then back to Damascus: but three years later he did go to Jerusalem, and he makes a point of saying that it was Peter whom he went to see and no one else (except in parenthesis, James the Lord's brother) (Gal. 1: 15 ff.).

Peter's vision of the Powers ordained of God, the archetypes of the nations, made him a specially suitable person for Paul to visit. Peter had seen them in the form of beasts, but they *were* the nations, who belonged neither to heaven nor entirely to earth: they were hung from the four points of the compass (or 'the four rulers'). We are reminded of Paul's condemnation of the nations, who turned from the glory of God seen in creation 'to the likeness of mortal man and birds and quadrupeds and creeping things' (Rom. 1: 23): man too often stops short at the archetypes, artificially abstracted and isolated from each other, and fails to look through them to their Creator; he stops short at the Many, and fails to see the One, and so loses his primal balance.

There is a link between Peter and Paul, and a possibility that both are linked with the second temptation, especially if the second temptation in St. Luke is an expansion of St. Mark's

brief note: '. . . and he was with the wild beasts' (Mark 1: 13).
It may well be so, and a mutilated fragment from Oxyrhynchus,
otherwise incomprehensible, probably from the Gospel according to the Hebrews, gives support to this theory: I quote the
restoration by Professor H. G. Evelyn White:[8]

> (Judas) saith: (Who then
> are they that) draw us, (and when shall come)
> the kingdom that is in heaven? (Jesus saith)
> The fowls of the heaven (and of the beasts)
> whatever is beneath the earth (or upon the
> earth, and) the fishes of the sea, (these are
> they that) draw you: and the kingdom (of
> heaven) is within you: (and whosoever) knoweth
> (himself) shall find (it: and having found it)
> ye shall know yourselves, (that) ye are (sons
> and heirs) of the Father the (Almighty, and)
> ye shall know yourselves (that ye are) in (God
> and God in you).
> And ye are the city(?) (of God).
> (Judas the interrogator is 'not Iscariot'.)

If this saying is based on a genuine utterance of Christ, it confirms the importance of St. Mark's reference to the wild beasts,
and links them at once with Paul in Romans (1: 23 *supra*), and
at the same time with Peter's vision of the beast nations. As here
restored it suggests that Jesus warned His disciples against being
led astray by archetypal qualities, which He portrayed theriomorphically. Another restoration of the same saying, by
Lagrange (quoted by Dr. James on the same pages), is to much
the same effect, but lays more emphasis on the possibility for
good in the archetypes; they can draw those who know God
closer to an understanding of Him through an understanding of
self.

With all this in mind, and with the three synoptic accounts of
the second part of the Temptation before us (in St. Matthew,
placed third), we may see the Christ 'with the wild beasts', hung
on a point between heaven and earth to make His choice. It was
not merely a temptation to the way of power in terms of earthly
categories: it was a decision whether or not to abide by His
Father's plan. God had chosen the Jews, and it was to the Jews
that Christ had been sent; nor must He overstep the Divine

commission granted to Him. We make too little of the second
temptation unless we see how clearly Jesus must have foreseen
the difficulties of preaching to His own people. Just as a man
who has been dealing with his troublesome fellow-men turns
with relief to animals—the wildest of them more tameable than
the self-will of man—so Jesus was tempted to turn from the
religious genius of the Jews, no longer plastic but hard and self-
sufficient, to the hungry nations waiting to be fed.

But God's respect for rights is as scrupulous as it is astonishing.
Whether the rights are those of rebellious demons, or of a stiff-
necked chosen race, yet God remains faithful and cannot deny
Himself. This scrupulous respect for rights Jesus as scrupulously
observed. The Messiah did not turn to the Gentiles until His
own people formally took Him and handed Him over to them.
As King of the Jews He was crucified: as King of the Gentiles
He rose again. But in the meanwhile He would worship the Lord
His God, and Him only would He serve: and at this point I will
ask the reader to turn to Deuteronomy, chapter 8, and read
straight through to chapter 9, verse 17. Here is the very same
transition of thought, through the wilderness with its manna to
the promise of the good land: but the journey is over fiery serpents and scorpions, through nations great and mighty, through
the same temptation to stop short at the spirits of great and
mighty nations, and make them and their glory into God—and
so to worship the prince of this world.

So far then, St. Luke has kept in step with St. Mark's brief
summary. Finally, the devil took Jesus to Jerusalem. Was this a
descent to earth from the heights of vision?—a literal journey
still fasting across Jordan to the capital city? I think not. Jerusalem was not only a city, it was an idea. It was a name too high
for any oath: it was the city of the Great King. In it 'two kings
are struggling together to reign',⁹ and one invites the other to
cast himself down to earth and so fulfil the apocalyptic prophecies of the Messiah, who was to descend with an escort of
ministering angels.

But it was Satan, not Jesus, who was to fall as lightning from
heaven, at the triumph of the new seventy. Jesus was not to be
taunted into facing God with an 'Either—or . . .'. 'You claim
to be the Son of God,' said Satan, 'do you not trust Him?'

Moses in his day faced God with an 'Either—or . . .': he would strike the rock, for God would not let him down. Nor did God let him down. The water flowed, and the people drank: but those who tempt God cannot lead His children into the land of promise.

'And the angels ministered to him,' adds St. Mark laconically. Jesus had refused to claim their escort, and by His refusal had defeated their tyrant prince. By this He won their voluntary submission. By His concentration upon God Himself, higher than archetypes or angels, Jesus tamed the wild beasts; angels they had been created, and in their submission they returned to their angelic nature and to co-operation with God-in-man.

'But surely it was the Cross and Passion which won the submission of the Principalities and the Powers? At the Temptation the ministry had not even begun.' We continually find the Time process short-circuited in the gospel. The Temptation and the Passion are two points in time which touch, just as the Transfiguration touches the Ascension, and the Ascension the Parousia. Time can be overtaken; and during the '*ecstasis*' of the Temptation, time was overtaken and the lines of life were laid. Once more there was peace in heaven (as the Palm procession later cried), for the war had entered man's own country: the occupying forces were being attacked.

NOTES

[1] It was not until some time after hearing this myth from an aged Dagbana that I read the slightly different version in J. G. Frazer's *Folk-Lore in the Old Testament*, vol. I, p. 62.

[2] This normally means that the succession through male or female has been maintained in the priesthood.

[3] Lev. 17: 7; 2 Kings 23: 8—('high places of the gates' should be rendered, 'high places of the hairy ones'; *v.* Oesterley and Robinson, *Hebrew Religion*, p. 112); 2 Chron. 11: 15; Isa. 13: 21; 34: 14.

[4] The fallen angels have themselves a kind of departmental dominion, each over his own respective beast, which they have abused: *v.* Baruch. 3: 16.

[5] Midrash Tehillim to Ps. 91: 5; *v.* Oesterley and Robinson, *Hebrew Religion*, pp. 111–21.

[6] R. H. Charles, *The Book of Enoch*; *v.* espec. pp. civ, cv.

[7] This passage is quoted by Prof. T. W. Manson, *The Sayings of Jesus*, p. 43.

[8] M. R. James: *The Apocryphal New Testament*, pp. 26 ff. H. G. Evelyn-White: *The Sayings of Jesus from Oxyrhynchus*. Note also Swete's rendering of another gospel fragment, in M. R. James, op. cit., p. 29, footnote.

[9] Origen, quoted by T. W. Manson, op. cit., p. 45.

Chapter 10

GALILEE OF THE NATIONS

A. THE GOSPELS

'AFTER I am raised up, I will lead you forward into Galilee'
(Mark 14: 28). Upon that phrase, overheard by a young man
in a linen cloth on the Mount of Olives, the gospel of the Resurrection turns. The shepherd was to be smitten and the sheep
scattered (Mark 14: 27). But follow up the quotation, from
Zechariah 13: 7-9:

> It shall come to pass, that in all the land, saith the Lord, two
> parts therein shall be cut off and die; but the third shall be left
> therein. And I will bring the third part through the fire, and will
> refine them as silver is refined, and will try them as gold is tried:
> they shall call on my name, and I will hear them: I will say, It is
> my people; and they shall say, The Lord is my God.

In that key phrase which follows the quotation, which is a
reminder of the whole passage, the apostles were told which
part was that 'third part' which was to be refined and tried. It
was Galilee—Galilee of the nations.

It has been suggested that it was that same young man, early
at the tomb, clad this time in a white robe, who in the dimness
of the empty tomb was taken for an angel by the three visiting
women.[1] Without any intention of masquerade, he passed on
what he had heard on the Mount of Olives, and the meaning
which the empty tomb had given to it. But the message was not
given, at least not for a considerable time, for they were afraid.
We may take leave to doubt whether it was ever properly
heard, except by John Mark who spoke.[2]

It was, I think, Dr. Burkitt who suggested that it was in an
attempt literally to follow those instructions that Peter met the
risen Master, and was turned back to Jerusalem; and that that
was the original of the '*Quo vadis?*' legend. But that theory, attractive enough, becomes attended with so much difficulty

when we find Peter with six others actually in Galilee within a fortnight (John 21), that it seems unlikely to be true.

There is no reason to believe that Peter was ever willing, or indeed able, to give an account of the appearance to him which took place on Easter afternoon. It seems easier to suppose that the message about Galilee was eventually given, but not until more than a week later; that the seven apostles then set off for Galilee and were there made to realize something of what Galilee meant.

What Galilee had mostly meant to them was *fish*; and it is characteristic of the proper Christian approach that it was through fish that the Risen Christ shewed the Apostles its spiritual meaning. There was another miraculous catch, with a difference from the early one recorded by St. Luke (5: 1–11): on this occasion the catch was never shipped, the fish were counted carefully, and the nets were intact. Another remarkable thing was that although they were bidden to bring of the fish which they had caught, those fish were not cooked and eaten: they were invited as guests to a meal of bread and fish provided by Christ Himself, as Sir Edwyn Hoskyns points out (*The Fourth Gospel*, vol. II, pp. 660 ff., ad loc.). He also makes the symbolism of the number, a hundred and fifty-three, unmistakably clear. The fathers explained the number in various ways: the important thing about their explanations is that they all agree upon the meaning of the number, which signified the universalism of the gospel, which was for all nations. Anti-types of this are Matthew 13: 47 f., the parable of the drag-net which 'gathered of every kind'; and the important passage from Ezekiel (47: 9–12) (*vide* Jerome's commentary ad loc.). The meal of bread and fish was symbolic of the Eucharist—'In primitive Christian Eucharistic iconography fish are often substituted for wine' (Hoskyns, op. cit., p. 664). The Gentiles were thus invited to the Christian Eucharist in Galilee of the nations.

Galilee, like Jerusalem, was more than a geographical name: it was an idea. Dr. R. H. Lightfoot discussed this in his *Gospel Message of St. Mark* (p. 106 ff.), though I would go further than he does in the matter of its meaning. The Galilee to which Jesus promised to lead His disciples forward could not be marked on any map; it is perhaps my fault that I have not found in any commentator, ancient or modern, its full significance set out, except by implication in Sir Edwyn Hoskyns.[3]

Dr. Lightfoot has suggested that St. Mark's gospel ended as it now ends, at Chapter 16, verse 8, and that St. Mark described no Resurrection appearances because they were indescribable (op. cit., p. 96). But that does not mean that the appearances were not fact in the truest sense. They were more, not less, real than our day-to-day experience. The risen Lord was touched and handled, He spoke and walked, He cooked and ate fish. The appearances were *real* appearances to men and women who were only on the way to becoming real; for Jesus was leading them forward into Galilee.

Here at last St. Matthew's gospel may help us (28: 16–20). Angels or John Mark first, and then Jesus Himself sent the message about Galilee to the brethren; and the eleven disciples went (when they got the message) into Galilee, as they were bidden, to the mountain where Jesus had appointed them. But what mountain was this? We read of no mountain appointed for the meeting. Let us read on. They went, and saw, and worshipped, but some doubted: the only doubter whom we know doubted in Jerusalem, and was there convinced. But Jesus came and spoke to them, and said: 'All authority hath been given unto me in heaven and earth.'

The words have a curiously familiar ring. Where did someone say something like that before?—and, according to St. Matthew, on a mountain, too? 'All these things will I give thee, if thou wilt fall down and worship me.' Or, more strikingly, from St. Luke, 'To thee will I give all this authority, and the glory of them: for it hath been delivered unto me; and to whomsoever I will give it.'

Galilee of the nations was an idea, or if we speak in cosmic terms a place where Jesus was with the 'wild beasts', who were the spirits of the nations: by refusing the offer of authority, He received their submission in anticipation. Can St. Matthew have thought of all this? At least his next sentence suggests it: 'Go ye *therefore*, and make disciples of *all the nations*, baptizing them . . .'

Galilee of the nations was no new idea: and if Jesus spoke in riddles, it was not the first time that He had done so, as a reference to 'Galilee' in a big New Testament concordance will shew: the mere reading through of quoted passages is impressive enough, and shews that Galilee means more than geography.

After all, then, Jesus received as a right the authority He had refused to bargain for; and by that right His servants were free to make known to all nations the mysteries of the Kingdom of God, so that through them the Principalities and Powers also might know and be redeemed (Eph. 3: 10).

B. THE ACTS

It was only logical, therefore, that the first gift of the Holy Spirit should be the gift of tongues: the Church was given the power to put into effect the command of its risen Master. It may have been an actual speaking of languages which took place: it may have been some sublime form of utterance, the highest common factor of all languages, which penetrated below the conscious level of understanding and immediately touched the intuition of hearers. There is no doubt that communication was established in some way which all recognized as supernatural and amazing. It was something far more fundamental than common prophetic frenzy or the later degenerate glossolaly, which could hardly have converted three thousand hearers on the spot; nor could it later have induced a trained wonder-worker to offer money so as to learn the trick (Acts 8: 18). It is perhaps significant that the hearers exclaimed, 'Behold, are not all these which speak *Galilaeans*' (2: 7). The same St. Luke, who was careful to explain away the phrase 'I will lead you forward into Galilee', faithfully reported this saying without apparently realizing its significance.

It was not at once that the early Church realized the fulness of the mystery. It was a hard lesson for Jews to learn that *the nations* did not merely mean Jews and proselytes of the Dispersion. First, Samaritans were included; then a Roman centurion; then, to the dismay of John Mark, Paul and Barnabas consorted freely with Gentiles of Perga (if we may so understand Acts 13: 13); finally the Church sanctioned the inclusion of Gentiles freely and on the same footing as Jews (Acts 15). But it remained a mystery past the understanding of many Jewish Christians.

C. St. Paul

To St. Paul it was clearly the greatest mystery of all. He explained its meaning carefully to the Roman Christians (11: espec. verse 25; *vide* also 16: 25). The message was rejected by the Jews: the Divine dispensation used this rejection for the bringing in of the nations; but final salvation still waited upon the conversion of the chosen people. The gospel was a stumbling block to Jews and foolishness to philosophers: it was the mystery of God and the power of God, hidden from the heavenly archons who crucified Christ (1 Cor. 1 and 2: 1–16). But the predetermined purpose of God, made known in the mystery of His will, was to sum up all created things in Christ—not the nations only (Eph. 1: 9 ff.). And 'all created things' meant not only things on earth, but 'principalities and powers in heavenly places', who had been brought to submission by direct proclamation (*vide infra*), but were to be *evangelized* through the nations of the world, who were themselves being evangelized by the Church (Eph. 3: 1–13; Col. 1: 25–9).

D. 1 Peter

The clearest exposition of the doctrine of the descent into hell is in this letter, Chapter 3: 18 to 4: 6. Christ was 'put to death in the flesh' and rejected by the Jews, but 'given life in the Spirit, in which He went and made proclamation to the spirits in prison'. No one who has read the Ethiopic Enoch can doubt that these are the angels who apostatized, as the patristic evidence testifies (Appendix, sec. C), supported by Dr. E. G. Selwyn (*The First Epistle of St. Peter*, comm. ad loc., and pp. 322 f.).

Eight souls had been saved by a kind of foreshadowing of Christian baptism. Baptism is not a denial of the 'flesh' side of the sacramental pattern, but the answer of a good conscience to God through the 'spirit' side, that is the resurrection of Christ; this involves the acknowledgment of Him as supreme over angels and authorities and powers (3: 18–22).

The flesh is inseparable from the Christian pattern. Christ suffered in *flesh*: our intention must be to do the same, for suffering accepted in *flesh* means an end of sin: it means living the rest of our *life-in-flesh* in the atmosphere of the will of God instead of the desires of men: here Peter surely had in mind the time when Jesus turned on him as the spokesman of Satan, who minds 'not the things of God but the things of men'.

With three hammer blows—the word *sarki* three times repeated—Peter drove home the lesson that for Christians there is no escapism. The almost brutal sacramentalism of the Christian gospel could not appear more clearly than in this passage, which begins with spirits in prison and ends with the evangelization of the dead. The dead were evangelized, so that though they had been judged by human standards in the flesh, they might live according to God's standards in the spirit. 'Judged' is aorist subjunctive, 'live' is present subjunctive: the change in tense shows that Peter was speaking of the literal dead, not of men and women 'dead' in sins. For the 'dead' who were evangelized were those who had not had their chance: human values had assessed them and had wrongly condemned them: God's values gave them life in the Spirit.

The imprisoned Powers, on the other hand, who had once been faithless, with every chance of knowing God's will and purpose, had the proclamation made against them (3: 19). Christ 'put off from himself the principalities and the powers' and 'made a show of them openly, triumphing over them in it' (i.e. the Cross) (Col. 2: 15); their redemption still waited, and meanwhile their tyranny was at an end. As shepherds they had been faithless; their misjudged flock had the gospel preached to them, and were given the opportunity of life in the Spirit (1 Pet. 4: 6). It remained for the Church to redeem even those faithless Guardians of the nations, by a living gospel preached to those (yet living) who were their representatives on earth: their reconciliation was already foreshadowed in their submission to Christ.

E. The Fathers

'Seen of angels, proclaimed to nations.' Angels who had 'deserted the beauty of God for a fading beauty, and fell from heaven to earth with so great a fall' (Clem. Alex., Paed. Bk. III, ii, 14) belonged now by their own choice to the *flesh* side of the sacramental pattern. The nations their charges (id., Strom. VI,

17, 822 P), enslaved and dead (id., Protr. I, 4P-Stahlin, 1905), received the gospel: and by their posthumous acceptance of it they entered the *spirit* side of the pattern. In the 'proclaimed' of this second pair of the mystery-creed there is this double significance: for the 'spirits in prison' it was a proclamation that their tyranny was at an end; for the enslaved souls it was the sign manual of their freedom.

The proclamation meant freedom not only for the departed of the nations, but also for their living successors. Those of the living nations who accepted Christ were taken from the care of the angelic archons, with the chosen people, into the care of God (1 Clem. Rom., 29: Lightfoot, p. 20 f.). By the reconciliation made between visible and invisible orders of beings—the restoration of *kosmos*—the ranks of heaven were made glad and the ills of earth were healed (Hippol. c. Ber. et Hel. P.G. 10, p. 833; also p. 857). The gates of heaven were opened by the Powers at the sight of Christ *in flesh* ascending as King of Glory (Hippol. on Ps. 24, P.G. 10, p. 609).

There is no need to multiply references to show how fully the Fathers accepted the New Testament teaching of Christus Victor. A few selected references will be found in the Appendix, sec. C. But that teaching was unquestionably of the 'esse' of the faith. Jesus had led His people forward into Galilee of the nations. He had defeated the tyrants and freed the captives. He left it to His Church to continue His work and gather the nations in.

It may simplify the doctrine to sum it up in seven movements:

(1) Christ was rejected by His own people, and crucified by the world-rulers of this darkness—the fallen Guardians—in the sense that they were forced to stand by the results of what they had let loose upon the world in their fall.

(2) He died, and in the halls of death preached the gospel to His fellow dead.

(3) He was quickened, and in 'heavenly places' (i.e. not God's heaven but a lower sphere) made proclamation of victory to the fallen Guardians.

(4) He received authority over the nations, which He delegated to His Body on earth, the Church—which is thus inevitably a missionary Church in its very being.

(5) The fallen Guardians themselves were to receive the gospel by means of the preaching of the Church. [4]

(6) Man's dominion over nature was to be re-established through faith in the victory of Christ, and by means of the power which such faith provides.

(7) All was to be summed up in Christ, who would surrender it with Himself to the Father in filial obedience.

The last two movements belong to the final pair of the *homologia*, and to the next two chapters. We must now seem again to digress a little, to consider the whole pattern summed up in the Name which gave this power to faith.

NOTES

[1] There are only two passages in the New Testament where the word *'neaniskos'* is used. One is St. Mark 14: 51, *'neaniskos pĕribĕblēmĕnos sindŏna,'* 'a young man having a linen cloth cast about him'. The other is St. Mark 16: 5, *'neaniskon pĕribĕblēmĕnon stŏlēn leukēn'*, 'a young man arrayed in a white robe': Mark does not say that it was an angel—indeed there is no parallel in the Bible to this description of an angel as a young man, if that is what Mark meant. It seems more reasonable to suppose that he said a young man and meant a young man. And as he uses the same word and the same qualifying participle, it is at least possible that he is referring to the same young man, namely himself.

[2] The best chronology of the first Eastertide is in Westcott's introductory note to Chapter XX, in his great commentary on the fourth gospel.

[3] Since the writing of this chapter, the *Journal of Theological Studies* has published an article by the Rev. C. F. Evans (vol. V, Pt. I, new series, April 1954) under the title 'I will go before you into Galilee'. In it he points out that Sir Edwyn Hoskyns did in fact produce a study of this text, 'Adversaria Exegetical', published in *Theology*, Sept. 1923. This did not receive the notice it deserved, and was quite unknown to me. Mr. Evans's article follows up Hoskyns in interpreting Galilee symbolically and in the same sense as I have done. I am proud to have such distinguished support. Both articles repay study.

[4] This may seem to be in conflict with the account of the temptations. But only if finite time-sequence is taken as governing supra-temporal orders. It is the old business of *Chronos* versus *Kairos*.

Chapter 11

FAITH IN HIS NAME

A NAME may have its extension. The simple name of Jesus of Nazareth was at first enough for those who had known Him or known of Him. It was used for healing (Acts 3: 16) and for exorcism (19: 13 ff.), and misused. It was also used for baptism (19: 5), which was healing, cleansing and exorcism too. Because it was misused, it had to be safeguarded and extended; and a very early form of confession of the Name is that of the Ethiopian eunuch as we have it in our Authorized Version. The confession did not perhaps belong to the original story, but its importance as an early confession remains (Acts 8: 17), and is supported by the epistle to the Hebrews (4: 14) and the first epistle of St. John (4: 15): 'I believe that Jesus Christ is the Son of God.'

There is earlier evidence for a more usual variant, the confession that 'Jesus Christ is Lord' or 'Jesus is Lord', which we find in the first epistle to the Corinthians (12: 3), the epistle to the Romans (10: 9), and the epistle to the Philippians (2: 10 and 11). In his *Earliest Christian Confessions*, Professor Cullmann gives it as his view that there grew out of this confession that Jesus (Christ) was Lord the acknowledgment that all powers in heaven, earth and under the earth were subjected to Him (pp. 55, 61).

In these two simple forms of confession there are the same three basic ideas as in the three pairs of the *homologia*. (1) Jesus, the human Saviour who revealed in flesh the saving power of God—vindicated in the Spirit. (2) Christ, anointed with power, seen and dreaded by demons, seen and acknowledged by angels fallen and unfallen, proclaimed to the principalities. (3) The Lord, supreme over all creation—and its anchor through faith, enthroned as King and Judge in evident glory.

These brief and positive confessions contained the seeds of

79

what the *homologia* sets out in balanced couplets: the *homologia* added the important emphasis upon the sacramental nature of Christianity, which I have called the flesh-and-spirit pattern; and it added this without losing the essential simplicity of the Faith-in-the-Name which achieved such remarkable things in the early days. It remained a Christ-centred confession. It is Jesus who revealed God in the flesh, and whose revelation was vindicated as truth in Spirit, in Baptism, Resurrection and Pentecost. It is Jesus Spirit-anointed, the Christ, who was recognized by demons and angels, who controlled them with the word of power, cast them out when in unlawful possession with the finger of God; who was proclaimed on earth as King in letters of Greek and Latin and Hebrew for all nations to read, and to the Guardians in the halls of death as their conqueror. It is Jesus the *Kyrios*, the Lord, who is still touched by the faith of creation as He was touched on earth by the hands of desperate men and women; who Himself is linked with the High and Holy One in His ascended glory.

Meanwhile, the sacramental balance removed the need for Christological quibbling. One hypostasis or two? How closely were the two natures linked? Which nature predominated, and how? And when these questions have been answered, what is the effect upon Eucharistic doctrine and practice? Jesus Christ was no philosophical synthesis: He was above and beyond philosophy, which does no more than tread the courts of the Gentiles: He belongs to the Holy of Holies. He was the Christian Mystery, whose meaning is something revealed—not discovered. He was tempted as we are. How can that be? Because He was man, in human flesh. How could He heal lepers, still storms, multiply loaves, turn water to wine, control frenzies, forgive sins? Because He was God. Was He alternately man and God? In the presence of the Mystery a question such as this has no meaning: there is no *alternately* with God—no 'first this' and 'then that'. For God, and potentially man, too, is beyond nows and thens: He is Lord of history. For history is written to shew, not man's dealings with man, but God's dealings with man. God speaks in history, and Jesus Christ the Lord is the Word spoken.

But man was separated from God in being separated from

his potential self. He had achieved independence and lost Life. Christ the God-man, Mystery and Sacrament, bridged the gap for those who renounce independence and apparent life, and choose real Life.

Has Jesus then done away with the need of mediation in man's approach to God? No; for man remains fallen and cannot approach the Holy One direct. By names and spells and incantations man had (without Christ) approached Powers higher than himself, which possessed a kind of infernal validity but did not lead to God. In Christ man has the only Name by which God may be approached. Christianity knows of no short cuts to God. The mediator is Jesus, Christ, Lord; and the Name is fairly set out as the Mystery of godliness—manifested in flesh, justified in spirit—seen of angels, proclaimed among nations—believed on in creation, received up in glory.

Almost all important heresies to-day begin with the failure to see Christ as the centre of the creed. 'Yes, I believe in God, and am sure that His spirit and purpose inspire the world: Jesus was the greatest religious leader to realize that truth.' Or, 'Jesus was God, and as God he knew and could do everything: he could not have gone wrong.' Or, 'The flight of the alone to the Alone is what I believe in.' Or simply, 'Live a good life, and take Jesus for your example, and stop theorizing.' Neither spiritual inspiration nor ungoverned mysticism nor good works after an example can take man to God: but 'I believe that Jesus Christ the Lord is the Son of God' includes the whole doctrine of the Trinity, and the sacramental balance of the mystery-creed adds the necessary corollary of the fall of creation and its return to God's purpose through obedience, and faith.

It is not the Name, unqualified, which saves: it is 'his Name through faith in his Name'. The Name itself has efficacy and is the *spirit* side of the saving grace: faith in His Name releases and directs the latent power. It cannot too often be said that the sacramental approach is an approach from two directions: it is neither an overtaking nor a unilateral approach: it is meeting.

Faith is on the *flesh* side of the pattern, because Christian faith

is not bare belief or passive acceptance; it is the forward movement of surrender. The Communist philosophy lays it down
that a man's faith is seen in what he does, and not in what he
professes. Christ only so modifies that stern ruling as to say that
a man's faith is seen in what he continually aims at doing: we
are not pragmatists. 'I believe, help thou mine unbelief,' was
good enough for the most difficult miracle which St. Mark reported—the miracle which was both death and resurrection,
and which had defeated the disciples (Mark 9: 14–29).

This kind of faith, expressed in action, is sacramental faith
and can be directed only towards God sacramentally revealed,
Jesus Christ our Lord. For there is no other name under
heaven which is a valid object of faith. The Name cannot be by-
passed. Any attempt to by-pass it becomes one of two things,
escape or idolatry. Vedantism is the purely spiritual approach,
which subtly objectifies Spirit in the act of resignation and in
passivity.

Idolatry, on the other hand, is the expression of a misdirected
faith *which demands to see God in a form in which He will not be seen.*
It was the sin symbolized by the Valentinians as the desire of
Sophia-Achamoth to know God. It was the sin represented in
the Old Testament in the Tower of Babel myth, and which
appears in the book of Enoch in the story of the angels who
taught, and the men who desired to learn mysteries—a story
which appears and reappears in the early Fathers. It is the
demand of man to discover God by his own effort, to think of
Him in a picture of man's own contriving. It ends in the isolation of the Universal into one or more particulars—the worship
of archetypes in their own right.

Yet it seems that man must think in pictures. The highly
idealized search for ethical perfection, pure goodness in the
abstract, has failed again and again. It failed in Greek philosophy; it failed in Rome, in China, and it is failing in Western
civilization of to-day.

Jesus, seen as Christ and Lord, was the gracious gesture of a
God who realized human limitations and yielded to human
desire, and shewed a picture of Himself in human colours. But
if one picture of God is true, all others are false. 'He that believeth on him is not condemned: but he that believeth not is

condemned already, because he hath not believed in the name of the only begotten Son of God.'

The Christian Church allowed itself to be driven by Gnostics from a Christ-centred creed, which approached Trinitarian truth through Christ the Mystery of godliness, into a creed in which logical sequence took priority over God's revelation of Himself. But the emphasis of Luther, of St. Paul, and indeed of the whole of the New Testament is right. Man can only approach God from where he stands. His gospel must be the gospel of Jesus Christ the Son of God, and 'he that confesseth the Son hath the Father also' (1 John 2: 23). His creed must be the creed of Jesus Christ who revealed the Father and was glorified by Him; who released the Holy Spirit, and is in turn revealed through Him.

Chapter 12

FROM FAITH TO GLORY

THE last chapter but one left Jesus 'free among the dead'. The dead themselves are not free. Primitive religion places them in the sacred spot, be it river, rock or mountain, where the pool of tribal life is latent. Their individual life is limited: in so far as any form remains to them, it is the form of a beast: in so far as they individually have life, that life is dependent on posterity. Unless they are fed with 'life-food' in sacrifices, their 'life' (i.e. their positive power for good) will dwindle; they will become dark and angry and demonic, full only of the spiteful magic-force which is not life.

Nor did the Jews regard death as giving any kind of freedom. Sheol was a place of half-life; and all but the Sadducees looked forward to a restored freedom in the body at the resurrection. The chief horror of Sheol was that it was a place of separation from God.

Jesus had maintained in Himself the contact between man and God. Death did not break it; His descent into hell was with power. In normal human beings the body alone is the effective instrument of power: even the mind is effective only through the brain, and every act of will becomes physical as soon as it emerges from the chrysalis of intention. Soul without body moves in its own pattern and cannot change it, because the link with God is snapped at death. Perhaps great and good men, pre-Christian saints, may be thought to have maintained even through death some kind of link with God: Jesus Himself may have suggested something of the kind when He spoke of the patriarchs as alive, and their God as the God of the living: if so, their life consisted in the promise of resurrection.

When the Psalmist spoke of his being *free* among the dead, it was because He 'had no help', 'Like the slain . . . whom thou rememberest no more; and they are cut away from thy hand.'

84

It was a freedom of a most unenviable kind, freedom from God, in fact anarchy and chaos; for God had no access to Sheol, until at last in Jesus the power of God passed through the grave and gate of death. The gospel was preached even to the dead. If we wish for a complete picture of contemporary belief, enlightened by the Christus Victor doctrine, we may suppose something of this kind. Those who had allied themselves with the power of evil in this world received a kind of ghastly revival after death, and were enlisted as demons. If they could find a vacant personality, they were free to take possession of it (Clem. Recog. II, 71, 72). Those who had neither chosen the kingdom of Beelzebub, nor attained to the 'third heaven' with the patriarchs, remained helpless in Sheol.

Such was the picture in the minds of our Lord's contemporaries; and such was also, in a great measure, the picture in our Lord's own gospel. Sheol no doubt had its ups and its downs: there were places of torment, and places of comparative rest. But at best it was a dead-alive sort of place, to be dreaded and shunned. This place (or condition) Jesus entered, and offered to the dead a choice—the same choice as He had offered to the living. Then in the power of His resurrection life, He rose again to earth and to the 'heavenly places'—the imitation heaven where the tyrant angels were pictured as ruling —and there the victory of Jesus Christ the Lord was proclaimed. He received the freedom of Space and Time. What did He do with that freedom?

One of our chief heresies to-day is to suppose that Jesus Christ was born, lived, suffered, died and rose again *only* for us men and for our salvation. On the contrary, 'God in Christ redeems man: man in Christ redeems nature.' The Powers to whom the proclamation of victory was made were not only spirits of nations: they were the 'angels who once were holy', God's agents in the re-creation of a fallen world.

We can never fully understand the theology of the Creation, unless we see it as a Re-creation. The world was without form and empty of meaning. The original rebellion of God's commissioned archangel had robbed it of form and meaning. But the Breath of Life stirred the formless elements, and out of chaos came kosmos. All that we know of God's method suggests that He always works through living and personal agents, who are at liberty to 'reply to Him in terms not dictated by Him'.

If such free beings were His agents in Re-creation, the Watcher story and the Babel story assume a new importance for Christian doctrine, as well as the Adam and Eve story.[1] They are the myths of the fall of World-soul, and they shew the futility of hope in salvation through knowledge. The world and the personal powers behind it exercised their right of choice in favour of Death and Change—a theme which appears again and again in the mythology of primitive religions.[2] But their choice was swayed by two things: the first, a passionate desire for *knowledge* or *beauty*: the second, the presence of a lying spirit in the Universe, who persuaded them not to believe that *satisfaction of desire meant death*.

The result was the coming of death, and the interruption of Re-creation. If the cosmic agents had believed God, the redemption of Chaos through Kosmos would have been uninterrupted. Kosmos, then, includes the whole universe, as pictured in the cosmology of the time: it includes the divinely commissioned agents, fallen though they may be: it does not include the principle of evil, who belongs to Chaos and disorder, although His original commission as 'prince of this world' still holds, until the victory of Christ abrogates it finally.

The submission of the fallen angels to Christ re-established order among men. That is to say, the archetypal categories were re-established, and it became the task of the Church to persuade men into them, as re-ordered in Christ.

I have spoken of the personal powers behind the world, and have implied that they are guardians not only of men and nations, but of the energies of nature. I am aware that I shall be accused of animism, and I shall be told that the Ethiopic Enoch, primitive religious belief throughout the world, and even contemporary Jewish belief of the time of Christ, do not give sufficient ground for holding a view which has been abandoned by all educated people. If that be said, it will be truly said. Nothing short of unquestionable New Testament support for it will do. Is there such support?

It is common practice among educated Christians neither to

discount the mighty works of Christ, nor to accept them altogether. We accept those which lie within our experience: indeed, we are exceedingly complaisant, and we go to the limits
of conceivable possibility. We have heard of wonderful 'faith
cures' in our own day: we will accept all the healings, even the
restoration of the man born blind. We have heard of apparently
dead men restored to life: we will accept Jairus's daughter, and
even Lazarus—perhaps with a mental reservation as to what
their 'death' really was. We have had personal experience of disordered minds and nervous systems restored to normality: we
will believe in all the exorcisms. But when we come to the
Nature Miracles, the stilling of the storm, the walking on
the water, the feeding of the multitudes, the earthquake and the
darkness, we reserve the right to explain them away. We will
say, 'God in Christ redeems man': if we are honest most of us
will refuse to say, 'Man in Christ redeems nature.'

It is just those nature miracles which proclaim that behind
the disorders of nature are hidden disordered personal energies
—actual beings.

St. Paul has something to say about this:

> The earnest expectation of the creation (*ktisis*) waiteth for the
> manifestation of the sons of God (i.e. the restoration of fallen
> men). . . . For we know that the whole creation groaneth and
> travaileth in pain together until now: and not only they, but our-
> selves also, which have the first-fruits of the Spirit, even we our-
> selves groan within ourselves, waiting for the adoption, to wit, the
> redemption of our body. For we are saved by hope. . . .

And at the end of the chapter he gives a list of 'creatures' who
are presumably those who still groan and travail, but await the
manifestation of the sons of God: they are death and life (in
antithesis), angels, principalities, powers, present events and
(fears for) the future, height, depth (i.e. heaven and the abyss).
These are the cosmic orders, and to St. Paul are personal: nor
does he give us any reason to suppose that in this great eighth
chapter of Romans he is putting forward an opinion of his own,
unsupported by Christ—a thing which he is most scrupulous to
do when necessary.

G

Man's dominion over nature was restored in Christ. It is an essential part of the gospel throughout the New Testament. If we cannot accept it, it is at least honest to admit that the doctrine is there. The fact is that man still continues to try to establish his dominion over nature, but through knowledge. Man still follows the fallen angels who taught men mysteries which they could discover by search. But human knowledge, like earthly beauty, is but fairy gold: the end of them both is death. They are good if their end is both clearly seen and consciously accepted: but death belongs to their very nature, and there is no road to dominion over nature through them. Even if dominion over 'nature' should be established through knowledge, man's own nature would return upon him and strike him down. Man still fails to see that belief in God can alone establish his dominion over God's creation.

'Believed on in creation.' The threads of belief were tied, somewhat loosely it might seem, to the created world in the persons of the disciples before the Ascension. John saw and believed: Thomas finally believed: promise of salvation was to the baptized believer: signs would follow and support believers: blessings are to those who have not seen and yet believe: those who believe will have life through the Name of Jesus.

The 'thread of belief' is no mere manner of speaking. It is not merely like the rope which gives a climber confidence. It is a living link between man and man; how much more between man and God. It binds the psycho-analyst to his patient, sometimes embarrassingly closely: for the surrender of personality to anyone less than God Himself is a form of slavery. But to *believe in* God (*pisteuein eis*), for instance in the fourth gospel, is the surrender of the personality to a *gnosis* which is not according to the flesh.

Such full surrender of the *spirit*, in men who through the *flesh* are linked with God's material creation, provides a bridge of two spans between men in the world, men in Christ, and God in Christ. So kosmos is re-established, mediating powers are made unnecessary (for Christians), while the very powers behind nature are subject to the prayer of faith uttered in the Name which has become a Word of Power.

The ante-Nicene Fathers had no doubt of the power of the

'Name believed on'. They challenged their official persecutors to
test its power: they offered them every opportunity to prove
their claims false—if they could. Justin Martyr claimed that
faith in Christ brought evil spirits into subjection (Dial.
LXXVI, 6; LXXXV, 2; CXXI, 3). It was at Christ Himself
that they trembled (ibid. XLIX, 8): it was faith therefore which
made Him present in person with power. The evil powers, said
Minucius Felix, confessed themselves demons '. . . as often as
they are driven from bodies by us with words and prayers
which torture and burn them' (Octav. XXVII, 5). Try us and
see, says Tertullian in effect, the gods when challenged by us
will themselves acknowledge that they are demons (Apol.
XXIII, 4 ff.). It was, he said, the Christians who by their
presence in the Empire protected it from evil possession, though
they claimed no reward (ibid. XXXVII, 9; *v.* also XLIII, 2;
XLVI, 5). Cyprian and pseudo-Cyprian wrote of the shrieks
and groans of demons when exorcised (ad Demetr. 14, 15; de
Grat. Dei, 5). The power of present faith, said Theophilus of
Antioch, is so great that a pagan who possesses oracular powers
—when exorcised—confesses the demonic origin of his powers,
and testifies to the true God (ad Autol. Ep. II, 8). Lactantius
said much the same (Inst. II 16; IV 27).

On one thing, too, all the Fathers are agreed. The only real
weapon left to the devil after Christ's victory is fear, the wrong
kind of fear which is the father of suspicion and despair and
panic. That kind of fear is the antithesis of faith. Whilst fear is
the right reaction of evil towards good, it is not the right reaction of good towards evil. It undermines all power, and is an
obstacle: 'Fear not', 'Be not afraid', 'Why are ye fearful', 'Fear
not, only believe'. One object of the Incarnation was 'that we
being delivered from our enemies, might serve Him *without
fear*'. The only fear which does not undermine power is the
right fear, the fear of God, which gives security, one of the most
clearly realized of the needs of present-day man.

The right fear, in fallen man, arises from the knowledge of
what will happen if he does the forbidden thing. If he does it in
spite of his knowledge and fear, the wrong kind of fear may
undermine his trust: if so, it has the nature of the diabolical
shudder (Jas. 2: 19), which is the fear of known consequences,

and not the proper approach of imperfection to Holiness. The right attitude is to face the fear and accept the consequences: in this way faith and trust can survive actual sin, and the continually failing sinner is made secure by faith accompanied by the right fear.

The right fear is akin to worship, which is one reason why fear of the Creator is right and of the creature wrong. Fear may bring acquiescence or resentment: it should bring acquiescence to God and goodness: it should equally bring acquiescence to the consequences of evil, pain and suffering in the Christian's own self—for the acceptance of the consequence of his own or someone else's evil robs the evil of its power: it should bring resentment towards the evil thing itself, so long as it is confined to that evil thing and not extended to the personality in which the evil is seen. The fear of God, the fear felt for a just ruler by his people, the disciplinarian fear, gives security. But the fear of men is generally associated with unreliability and unpredictability when they are together. God is unpredictable but reliable. If a human leader be that, his men will not be afraid. Most men are predictable but unreliable: they need careful treatment, but there need be no fear of them. No man is completely unpredictable and unreliable, but pure evil is both. Where God has been banished there is every reason for fear of the devil.

Faith is a living link between living creatures. It is not limited to persons. It can bind persons and animals as securely as it can bind man and God, and it should do so. It is not a one-way process: it can only bind at all if it binds in both directions. Faith in God is no exception: the faith of the disciples in Jesus was called out by His faith in them. He continued to trust them without reason, which gradually brought them to trust Him with every reason. The evidence of God's faith in us is freewill. Nothing so much helps us to choose right as the knowledge that God depends upon our doing so—and yet will not compel us. A man who will not trust his fellow-man seldom trusts God; and disorder is as often the result of too little faith in others as of too much.

'Believed on in Kosmos.' I have translated kosmos by 'creation' rather than 'the world', and have tried in a note to Chapter 13 to shew good reason for doing so. Kosmos means order and is the effect of mind upon matter: but it is not the visible order in the world which prompts our faith. There is a general sort of order to be seen, a grand plan which through an immense amount of destruction produces what biologists and others call progress: and that progress has in the past produced a pathetic kind of faith in some comfortably placed optimists. But that is not faith in kosmos. 'Kosmos' is created order: and the only created order which can produce genuine faith is that order of which God—revealed in Christ—is Creator. It is a Creation which transcends natural order: it is a great re-ordering: and faith in it looks not at what the world is, but at what it becomes in Christ. Even the 'signs following' are a legitimate ground of faith, if not the highest ground. If other things seem to fail, we may be forced to believe only 'for the very works' sake'.

Yet the 'signs following' (as far as healings were concerned) were themselves dependent on human faith. Not the elemental signs which exorcized either spirits of nature in the storm or evil spirits in men: they were straight fights between the 'finger of God' and the limbs of Satan. But the outward sign of healing was not shewn until it was believed in: once believed in and shewn, the sign is a ground for more faith, which therefore grows like the mustard seed. But the seed must be there before it can grow.

'Believed on in creation' is the phrase of the mystery-creed more relevant to our predicament than any other. Having believed in God, in the Incarnation, in the gift of the Holy Ghost, in a Church which dispenses or withholds a forgiveness which is not limited by death, and in a resurrection to eternal life, we have still not believed in any of these things until we have taken our stand uncompromisingly on belief in God's control of a fallen world *in spite of freewill*.

The attempt to rationalize the elemental powers is a bucket which will not hold the water of Christian baptism. Dr. J. C. Conybeare, in a series of articles on the 'Demonology of the

New Testament' in the *Jewish Quarterly Review* (vols. 8 and 9, of 1896–7) set out the dilemma. Did Jesus believe what was generally believed in His day? It would appear that He believed in bodiless demons, ruled by Satan, haunting desolate places: they caused disease and madness and told lies: they had names, and expressed themselves through possessed persons: they could pass from person to person, or into animals: they were behind the elements, which could be exorcized in the same terms as men: the chief mission of the Messiah was to rid men of these pests: when Satan was dethroned, the Kingdom of God would be established: for exorcism the Name of Jesus was infinitely more effective than any other name. Conybeare then asked two questions:

(1) Did Jesus believe these things? If so, what becomes of His spiritual omniscience?

(2) Was He only pretending? If so, what becomes of His honesty?

Conybeare's conclusion is that Jesus was honest, and did believe these things—and therefore was not spiritually omniscient (and therefore, He would leave us to conclude, not the Son of God).

There is another answer, which preserves both His omniscience and His honesty—but I believe only one. That is that Jesus did believe these things, and *that He was right*. There is no escape for believing Christians from a thorough and uncompromising supernaturalism. True faith is 'not seeing, and yet believing'. Gospel criticism has failed (though it tried very hard at times) to strain the miraculous out of the gospels. It has failed to strain out even the miracles which most embarrass us. Patchwork criticism has had its day, and the demand that we shall believe in the full pattern of the gospel is uncompromising.

This implies no kind of fundamentalism; but it does imply belief in the inspiration of scripture. Men are imperfect instruments both for receiving and for transmitting the Spirit. Our justification is by faith. The Christian Myth, Christian ritual, Christian ceremonial, display a pattern which is constant. They belong to the outward and visible side of a sacramental religion: they are *the Faith*, as Kosmos is the medium in which it finds expression—the right ordering of what is disordered.

That is the *flesh* side of the last couplet. But Kosmos on earth is Glory in heaven. This glory, however, was seen on earth: it was seen in glimpses and in a final historical demonstration—at least if we accept the Lukan account. I confess myself unwilling to escape the difficulties which arise from that account by assuming an Ascension (unwitnessed) on Easter afternoon, which appears to be the position taken up by some Christian scholars. [3] That solution creates more difficulties than it solves. The great forty days remain historically and doctrinally indispensable. During those days the apostolic Church was being held in tension between the flesh and spirit sides of the pattern. It was being taught the things concerning the Kingdom, but it had not yet entered the Kingdom. The sacramental pattern was not yet complete. 'I am ascending,' said the risen Christ to Mary Magdalene. Whilst He was in the flesh men might touch Him in the flesh—and by the touch obtain healing and exorcism of evil. By that touch faith was shewn in Him. After His Ascension men might touch Him in the Spirit, and *His Name through faith in His Name* would heal and exorcize, as physical touch (in faith) had healed before. But the forty days was a time of waiting upon God, as our Lord's own forty days in the wilderness were a waiting upon God; and as the second forty years had been for Israel a time of waiting until they had faith to enter the promised land. [4] During those days, there were foretastes of the sacrament, but no completed sacrament. At Emmaus He broke the bread, and in the breaking of it was made known. At the sea of Tiberias He provided bread, and a symbol of the spirit side of the sacrament in the form of fish. In the upper room He actually ate fish Himself, and proclaimed Himself a being with flesh and bones like other men: but even there the mention of *blood* was avoided. Similarly, during the earthly ministry, the two Messianic banquets were celebrated with bread and fish. Only at the Last Supper was the full sacrament celebrated, and after it Jesus announced that He would no more drink of the fruit of the vine, until He drank it new with His disciples in the Kingdom of God. That time had not yet come— 'I am ascending.'

I have already suggested that the flesh and spirit pattern appears in the sacrament of Holy Communion in the simplicity of the symbols, bread and wine, without any metaphysical subtleties about essence and accidents. The post-Resurrection meals bear this out. In them the spirit side was Christ Himself, in visible presence. After the Ascension, faith in the Presence must take the place of sight of the Presence: the touch of faith takes the place of the touch of the physical senses—and the sacrament is received by the believer in both kinds, flesh and spirit.

The Son of Man was being glorified, but the glory had yet to be revealed. Until the seed of faith had been securely planted, He could not be received up in glory. So that, although the pattern of the mystery-creed is doctrinal and sacramental, that is not to say that it is unhistorical. History is one of the creatures which have acknowledged Christ as Lord, that God may reveal His truth through it. The chronology of the pattern is therefore part of the revelation of truth.

What exactly was Jesus doing during those forty days? There is no reason for not asking such a question, but it may be one which can be only symbolically answered. He was travelling very fast through time, until He reached the end of history itself: and at the end, the disciples were also transported for a moment not out of time but to the end of time. Their faith in the risen Lord revealed to them the Son of Man on the clouds of glory, which is both Ascension and Parousia. This was no subjective vision: when Christ was raised from the dead He was already Lord of history: the times of men were in His hand, and He was bound only (as He had always been bound—as God is bound) by the eternal purpose and pattern: for God cannot deny Himself.

It is as unrealistic to tie the Ascension down to Easter afternoon, and to turn all the remaining appearances into post-Ascension ones, as it is to deny the validity of the sequence of history. The argument which uses the Easter evening gift of the Holy Ghost to shew that the Ascension had taken place, can only be used with eyes closed to the repeated pattern of Death-Resurrection during the earthly ministry. By the grace of God there is charismatic repetition at the heart of things. The Kingdom was seen by three men on a mountain after the first confession of faith, and in it was seen the Messiah who had ac-

cepted the confession and explained Himself as the suffering
servant. It was a foretaste of the Ascension, but it was not the
Ascension. So the gift of the Holy Ghost to the disciples was a
foretaste of Pentecost, but it was not Pentecost: it gave authority, but it was not until Pentecost that they received power. At
the Transfiguration, the choice of the way of sacrifice revealed
the glory of the image of God in the face of Christ: at the Ascension it was the fullness of glory. On Easter evening, the apostles
received the seal or image of the Spirit: at Pentecost He des-
cended with power from on high.

The gradualness of the Ascension is borne out in the teaching
of the Fathers. Here, for instance, are two who quote Psalm 24
to the purpose. First Hippolytus, on Psalm 24 (23) (P.G. 10, p.
609) says:

> He comes to the heavenly gates: angels bear him company; and
> gates of heaven are closed. For he had not yet ascended into the
> heavens. Now for the first time flesh is ascending and appears to
> the heavenly Powers. It is said therefore to the Powers by the
> angels who are running before the Saviour and [Lord, 'Lift up
> your heads, Rulers, and be lifted up, Gates of Eternity, and there
> shall come in the King of Glory.'

Then, Rufinus of Aquileia, commenting on the Apostles
creed (cap. 31; *Ascendit ad coelos*) says:

> Finally, since that entry was newly seen by the gate-keepers and
> Rulers, they spoke to each other as they saw the nature of flesh
> win its way into the secret places of the heavens, as David pro-
> claimed, full of the Holy Spirit, saying, 'Lift up your gates,
> Rulers, and be lifted up, eternal doors, and there shall enter the
> King of Glory.'

And later,

> The same David says also somewhere else (Ps. 48: v. 5), God has
> gone up with joyfulness, and the Lord with the blast of the trum-
> pet. For it is the custom of victors to return from battle with the
> blast of a trumpet.[5]

'Received up in glory.' That is, a Kingship not of this world,
but of the ages. Kingdoms of this world are mixed up with lust

for power, and lust for this and that else. Ambition, greed, fear, suspicion: all the world's kingdoms are full of intensity of emotion and desire. But the Kingdom of heaven is an ascended Kingdom. To it belongs true glory, and true glory has nothing to do with intensity of emotion: the very idea of ascension suggests lightness.

None the less, true Kingship possesses *power of the spirit*, and all the more so for shedding emotional intensity. It has the Master Touch, which gives flavour to the flavourless in life, power to the paralysed, sight to the blind, hearing to the deaf, sparkle to dull faces, the spring of youth to the heavy step of middle age. It has nothing to do with crimson faces, set teeth and heavy breathing. Every man, even Christ Himself, must feel intensity of emotion at times—must make efforts in a groaning and travailing world: but heavy intensity belongs to our kingdoms of this world and not to the Kingdom of heaven. 'Not by might nor by power, but by my spirit saith the Lord of Hosts.' Ascension is that which releases the Spirit, and Spirit is a light-hearted power, which bloweth where it listeth, and we hear the sound thereof, but cannot tell whence it cometh and whither it goeth.

We are inclined to think that there is some virtue in being what we call profound—which is more often being wilfully obscure. We think that—for instance—the joy of the love of man and woman lies in burning words quivering with suppressed passion. It does not. The real joy is in the light touch, not in the embrace 'locked lip to lip' in a kind of frenzy. And the laugh at oneself must never be far behind.

The experiments of Professor Rhine (*The Reach of Mind*), in the control of mind over matter, have revealed that the best control is obtained when the people involved treat the experiment as a sort of game. When Professor Rhine allowed his students to become intense and full of effort, control vanished.

Something may be seen of this in primitive religion. The best side of it is sometimes expressed in dances which do not grow gloomy and demonic, but which capture that elusive something which belongs to the world of fairy tales and folk-songs. Call it superficial, if you will: but it has a power which we recognize in J. M. Barrie and T. S. Eliot and the Pied Piper. Much that is

called profound and reckoned as important belongs not to
heaven but to the abyss.

And so the mystery-creed takes us back to the beginning
again, to that which is mystery in its true sense. It is a secrecy
which has nothing to do with gloom and obscurity, but which
is only secret because it is elusive. It rebukes Christians who
gaze fixedly into the heavens, seeking the joy which has un-
accountably vanished. It tells them that the joy will come
again unsought, as it vanished unexpectedly.

It is a fact of common experience that the most precious
moments are also the most elusive. There are strange sadnesses
which some find in an autumn morning, some in a sudden
scurry of wind and rain, some in the fugitive scent of a bonfire;
and they cannot be run to earth. They will bear neither close
approach nor careful examination. Most of us know creatures of
another world who are creatures of inadvertence, and have been
called by more names than there are languages. We have met
the students of their stories, ways, and habits, who by their very
intensity suck out their souls and leave them flat and lifeless as a
fishmonger's slab. We have heard the promising ghost story
ruined by over-accurate description.

God forbid that pen, ink or printing-press should try to
reveal to the wise and prudent mysteries meant only for those
who have kept their childhood, that those who wonder should
be schooled out of their wonder, to lose their reign and rest.
'And when the seven thunders had uttered their voices, I was
about to write: and I heard a voice from heaven saying unto
me, "Seal up those things which the seven thunders uttered, and
write them not." '

Not until there is time no longer will the seventh angel begin
to sound, and the mystery of God be finished. Meanwhile its
meaning is declared only in words of prophecy, in images and
parables—so that those who have eyes may see, and those who
have none, or will not use them, may walk on still in darkness.
Few of us are prophets or poets: we may have glimpses of the
mystery but our lips are sealed and our tongues are inarticulate.
But here and there we can point at those who have known and
experienced the half-meanings which are the best echoes of

heaven that this age can provide. Meanwhile we have the sacraments.

NOTES

[1] Read C. W. Formby, *The Unveiling of the Fall*; Genesis, Skinner, pp. 16 f., especially the footnote; *The Ideas of the Fall and of Original Sin*, N. P. Williams.

[2] Sir J. G. Frazer, *Folk-Lore in the Old Testament*, vol. I, ch. II, pp. 50–77.

[3] E.g. A. M. Ramsey, *The Resurrection of Christ*, pp. 86 ff. But cf. pp. 121–3. Dr. Ramsey keeps the Resurrection and Ascension distinct as theological truths, though he seems to me to lose the sacramental pattern by losing the sense of gradualness in the Ascension: a sacrament demands agreement between the truth expressed and its outward sign. He loses also the typological fulfilment in the second forty days, which balance the second forty years of Israel in the wilderness.

[4] The first forty days of the Temptations answered to the first forty years of Israel in the wilderness. At the end of those forty years, Israel rejected God: at the end of the forty days, Christ the new Israel accepted God's way and set out for the Promised Land. The old Israel served a second forty years to learn their lesson and be renewed in the rising generation—at the end of which they entered Canaan. Jesus Christ had accepted God, but the chosen people had again rejected God in Him, while the disciples had been faint-hearted: again, as of old, it was Joshua-Jesus alone who had preserved his faith in God—and the new Church, as the old congregation in the wilderness, had their period in which to learn the lesson from him—forty days in which Jesus spoke the things concerning the Kingdom of God. But Caleb was also faithful, who was no true Israelite but inherited his portion by virtue of his faithfulness. Is he perhaps symbolized by the centurion, with his striking confession of faith?—the first-fruit of the Gentiles?

[5] Read also Tertull. Scorp. 10; Iren. c. Haer. IV, 13; Gosp. of Nicod., Pt. II, 5(21), A-N. Fathers, p. 203, 173.

Part III

PATTERN OF THE TRUTH

Chapter 13

ANTIPHONAL BALANCE

At first sight it might be said that even if all that has been said about the mystery-creed be true, it is still surprising that it is only found once in the epistles of the New Testament.

But it is in fact found twice; the second time is in the first epistle of St. Peter 3: 18 ff., where the form is slightly different, but the similarity of pattern is unmistakable. The Lord's Prayer itself is also only found twice in the New Testament, and then in different forms: yet no one would deny that its pattern was fundamental: and a moment's thought will remind us that it also has a two-element pattern, and carries the attention of the Christian who uses it backwards and forwards from heaven to earth, from God to man, from spirit to flesh.

And the *pattern* of the Lord's Prayer does appear time and again, not generally as a whole but in parts: there are prayers for bread, for forgiveness, for guidance and protection: there are records of miracles sacramentally shewing God's provision of those very things: there is teaching to shew what is the right order of importance—first the glorifying of God's Name, and then the neighbourly action—the Kingdom first and God's righteousness, and then the duties of a citizen—first the search for His will, and then the daily anxieties with the sting taken out of them.

If that is true of the Lord's Prayer, it ought equally to be true of our creed form. We ought to find the pattern recurrent in the New Testament, but not always as a whole: here a clause, there an antithesis, sometimes an echo of the words themselves.

Searchers of the Scriptures are always suspect. Holy writ has been an instrument to every man's hand and strange things have been proved from it. None the less to say that there are no thought patterns in it, no doctrines in embryo, no guidance in matters supernatural, is counsel of despair. Those patterns which, for instance, Dr. Farrer has seen in the Apocalypse and in the gospel of St. Mark may not be evident to all eyes: but to fail to see a thing is not to say it is not there, as every pathologist knows. We all see some of the patterns of the typologists, and reject the ones that we cannot see: but there is almost always something in what they tell us which the most hard-headed will admit. The human mind is a strange thing, and the psychologists (Dr. C. G. Jung, for instance) ask us to believe in stranger and more far-fetched types and patterns than the theologians (Dr. Farrer, for instance). The important thing is that there must have been a pattern, not whether St. Mark or St. John consciously realized it. Ultimately all patterns are either divine or demonic: it is a matter of urgent necessity to discover which are which.

It is for me to shew first what the pattern is, as will be done in general outline in this chapter; then when we know what to look for, to shew how that pattern (not necessarily this creed form itself, which was only taking shape) appears in the accepted writings of the early Church of the first century. There is no denying that Christians did think along these lines; the pattern would not appear clearly in two places in the New Testament otherwise: the question is, how fundamental was it to Christian thought?

There is no real reason then to expect to find it quoted in full again. And there are in fact two particularly good reasons why it should not have been quoted: first, that so long as it was important to the Church it was a secret; second, that it was soon superseded by Trinitarian and historical creed forms because it was thought dangerous. (How many good things the Church has given up because they are 'dangerous'!)

In an article in *The Thinker* (No. 5, 1895, p. 419), Prebendary B. Whitefoord says,

The creed was secret—secret because of the dangers of persecution. The creed was orally taught to the catechumens: just before baptism took place came the *Traditio Symboli*; this was followed later by the *Redditio*. But the secrecy of the rule of faith was consistently maintained, even when the danger of persecution was less imminent. It is curious to observe the emphasis laid upon this point by such early commentators upon the creed as Rufinus of

Aquileia and St. Augustine.[1] In stating the fact of the secret character of the creed, they seem almost to have forgotten the reason for it in the past.

I have already quoted (in Chapter 2) from Augustine and Jerome and Rufinus[2]—who are themselves echoing St. Paul's phraseology (2 Cor. 3: 3), who is himself echoing Jeremiah (31: 33) and Ezekiel (11: 19 and 36: 26)—but who are all applying that phraseology to an established tradition of the Church.

The creed is a deposit in the heart, and so a *mystery*. It is solemnly given in trust (*parathēkē*,[3] 1 Tim. 6: 20): it is a model for Christian teaching (*tupos*: Rom. 6: 17), though its truths may be elementary (*ta stoicheia*: Heb. 5: 12): it is the beginning of a rule of life (*kanōn*: Gal. 6: 16): it is recited together by initiates (1 Tim. 6: 12): it is traced back to one source only, and that is Christ (Heb. 6: 1), and is a pattern of sound doctrine[4] (2 Tim. 1: 13).

Early confessions were also more positive.

> We must allow (wrote Dr. C. H. Turner) for more of a positive element in the earlier stages of the Creed than in the later: there was more of the desire to embody in brief compass the most fundamental heads of the Church's own belief; less, as yet, of the intention to erect sign-posts of warning against the deviations of heresy (*Use of Creeds and Anathemas in the Early Church*, p. 15).

None the less, the early type of confession was superseded: anti-heretical warnings were needed, but it is a pity. And by the time that the canon of the New Testament was established, the inclusion of what had been a formula for Christians and initiates only was no longer indiscreet.

But even before that time we should expect to find in Christian documents the pattern of which the *homologia* was the summary, if it did really sum up for Christians of Asia Minor the Gospel which they preached.

First then, to examine the pattern. It is both horizontal and vertical, and has many implications which are easily missed.

It is composed of three couplets, not of two triplets.[5] The more usual opinion that it forms two triplets is based on a supposed lack of connexion or balance between the third and fourth lines: but they are in fact closely connected, as has been shewn. The pattern will be most clearly seen if the reader can imagine the sextet sung antiphonally (*'in vicem'* as Pliny says):

Officiant: Great is the Mystery of godliness, who was—

V. Manifested in flesh,	*R. Justified* in spirit,
V. Seen of angels,	*R. Proclaimed* among nations,
V. Believed on in creation,	*R. Received up* in glory.

If we read the words in italics vertically, we shall at once see the credal sequence. On the left hand side—the 'flesh' or outward-and-visible side—Christ is confessed as manifested, seen, believed on. On the right-hand side—the 'spirit' side—He is confessed as justified (i.e. vindicated), proclaimed, received up —a sequence of actions performed on His behalf by God.

The first sequence concerns created beings: in the second sequence it is God who acts each time, and His action is not within the realm of sense-perception; the qualifying terms are ideal, including the word 'nations' as has been shewn in the relevant chapter.

Reading horizontally we shall at once see the balance between the verbs in pairs: manifested-justified: seen-proclaimed: believed on-received up. God may be shewn, but what we need is that the demonstration be proved genuine: can this be God? God may be seen and still ignored, unless He proclaim Himself in power. God may be trusted in unquestioning faith, but the very faith itself looks forward: there must be sure and certain hope—a more solid spirit than the pale spectre which generally answers to the name—the hope of God's final vindication of Himself: He must be received up.

And now the nouns:

V. Manifested in *flesh,*	*R.* Justified in *spirit,*
V. Seen of *angels,*	*R.* Proclaimed among *nations,*
V. Believed on in *creation,*[6]	*R.* Received up in *glory.*

In the nouns again we see an ascending sequence: on the outward-and-visible side, Flesh (mankind); Angels (who are visible to, though not always seen by, men and animals); Creation (including the outward forms of principalities, powers, departed souls, fallen angels, and the visible world). On the inward-and-spiritual side, Spirit; Nations (which are ordained and constituted of God, Deut. 32: 8, a spiritual idea);

H

Glory. In this second sequence, the connection may not immediately appear to us; but it would certainly do so to a Jew. Isaiah 66: 15–19, gives the accepted picture of the Day of the Lord:

> V. 15. For behold the Lord will come with fire, and His chariots shall be like the whirlwind; to render his anger with fury, and His rebukes with flames of fire . . . (*spirit* symbolized).
> V. 18. I come to gather all nations and tongues (*nations*); and they shall come and shall see my glory (*glory*).
> V. 19. And I will set a sign among them (*spirit*), and I will send out from among them men who have been saved (LXX) to the nations . . . to the isles afar off, that have not heard my fame (*nations*), neither have seen my glory; and they shall declare my glory (*glory*) among the nations.

The classic picture of the Day of the Lord, in Joel 2: 28 ff., follows the same pattern:

> And it shall come to pass afterward, that I will pour
> out my spirit   (*spirit*)
> upon all flesh;   (*nations*)
> and your sons and your daughters shall prophesy, your old men shall dream dreams, your young men shall see visions:
>   (*glory*)
> and also the servants and the handmaids in those days will I pour out my spirit.   (*spirit*)
> And I will shew wonders in the heavens and in the earth . . .
> before the great and terrible Day of the Lord come.
>   (*glory*)
> And it shall come to pass, whosoever shall call on the Name of the Lord shall be saved: for in Mt. Sion [LXX reading] and in Jerusalem shall the saved one be as the Lord has said, and they that have glad tidings preached to them, whom the Lord has called.
>   (*nations*)

And indeed the association of the three ideas pervades the closing chapters of Isaiah (especially 60; 61; 64: 1–3). The 'servant' passages are full of the sequence: a striking example is 42: 5–8 (cf. also Ezek. 39: 21–9). These predictions are fulfilled in the Church at Pentecost. The gift of the Spirit immediately opens the mouth of Its receivers: they speak in terms which all nations can understand: the barriers have been broken, and the

curse of Babel has been abolished; communications have been
re-established. The disciples have already received their commission; in the gift of the Spirit they receive power to carry it
out. So the nations are shewn the Glory. All these things are the
action of God, who works through charismatic channels and
human agents. So to the Christian the sequence makes sense.

There is a horizontal parallelism between the nouns, as between the verbs:

(a) *Flesh* and *Spirit* are the headings to the two columns.

(b) *Angels* and *Nations* we have seen to be balanced, in the
    Jewish and early Christian concept of angel guardians of
    the nations. In this connexion it is interesting to read
    Dr. C. G. Jung's *Essays on Contemporary Events*.

(c) *Creation* and *Glory* are balanced: the glory of God is seen
    in an ordered creation, and in Perfect Man, its end and
    purpose. *Creation* is the 'flesh' side of this pair, though the
    concept includes much which we should call spiritual. It
    is flesh, because it belongs still to the order of fallenness
    or imperfection.

There is also an historical order in these pairs. Time and
history are valid for Christians, though not eternally valid. The
Mystery is the proclamation that even in a fallen world, eternal
truths can be told. Jesus Christ revealed the whole truth, but
the understanding of it is limited by sin, not by any inherent
defect in the created world.

This then is the sequence, summed up in its pattern:

Manifested in flesh, justified in spirit—

Jesus the Man, living life as God intended, justified and vindicated in every miracle from Baptism to Ascension; put to death
in the flesh, Him God raised up.

Seen of angels, proclaimed among nations—

Christ witnessed by angels, seen as man was intended to be,
the climax of manhood; Man asserting his God-given dominion
over nature in the strength of God; universal man transcending
all barriers.

Believed on in creation, received up in glory—

Jesus Christ the Lord, man's only security; the foundation of
the Church, through which those who believe on him are Christ
Himself, His Body. As soon as the Church has been founded,

Christ has reached the end of time. Received up in glory, witnessed by the Church which will see Him come as it saw Him go. And the Ascension is no less an accomplished fact because we have not yet reached it.

Great is the Mystery of godliness—
Jesus—manifested in flesh, justified in spirit,
Christ—seen of angels, proclaimed among nations,
Lord—believed on in creation, received up in glory.

NOTES

[1] See Chapter II, and note (1) on that chapter: also see comments by B. Busch, *Ephemerides Liturgicae*, lii, 1938, 440 f.; and Kelly, *Early Christian Creeds*, p. 54 f.

[2] Cf. Irenaeus, c. Haer. III, 4, 2, P.G. 7, p. 855. Augustine, Rufinus and Jerome are not our earliest witnesses to the *disciplina arcani*. In the reference above Irenaeus is speaking of the oral tradition left behind by the apostles, which (he says) 'is preserved by the barbarians who believe on Christ, and who have their salvation written by the Spirit on their hearts without paper or ink, and who keep the ancient tradition carefully'. The creed form which follows is nearer to the Apostles' Creed than to our creed-pattern: but there is a faint flavour of it. (Cf. 2 Cor. 3: 3.)

[3] The Latin *depositum* translates this. See Chapter I. Irenaeus speaks of the apostles, who, 'as rich men into a *depositorium*, have filled it [the Church] full of everything which belongs to the truth'. This is a characteristic use of *depositum* (or a derivative of it), which itself suggests the *disciplina arcani*.

[4] These references to aspects of the creed I owe to the quoted article by Preb. Whitefoord. But cf. Parry, *Pastoral Epistles*, p. xcvii, who expounds this phrase otherwise.

[5] See the re-translation into Aramaic of this creed-form by Dr. W. E. Barnes, reproduced in F. H. Badcock, *The Pauline Epistles*, p. 134. The first couplet has lines of four syllables; the second and third have five-syllable lines.

[6] I add a list of uses of 'kosmos' without the definite article in the New Testament. In each instance the meaning 'creation' gives a more significant sense than 'the world': (t) is an exception to this.

(*a*) Matt. 13: 35 (from Ps. 78: 2). I will utter things hidden from foundation of creation (*apo kataboles kosmou*).

(*b*) Matt. 25: 34. Inherit the kingdom prepared for you from foundation of creation (same Greek).

(*c*) Luke 11: 50. That the blood of all the prophets, which was shed from foundation of creation, may be required of this generation (same Greek).

(d) John 17: 24. Thou didst love me before foundation of creation (same Greek, with preposition *pro*).

(e) Rom. 1: 20. For the invisible things of Him since establishment of creation are clearly seen (*apo ktiseōs kosmou*).

(f) Rom. 4: 13. Not through law was the promise to Abraham or to his seed, that he should be heir of creation, but through the righteousness of faith (*to klēronomon auton einai kosmou*).

(g) Rom. 5: 13. For until law, sin was in creation (*en kosmo(i)*).

(h) Rom. 11: 12. If their fall (i.e. the Jews') is creation's enrichment . . . (*ploutos kosmou*).

(i) Rom. 11: 15. If the casting away of them is creation's reconciling . . . (*katallagē kosmou*).

(j) 1 Cor. 3: 22. (For all things are yours;) whether Paul or Apollos, or Cephas, or creation, or life, or death, or things present, or things to come: all are yours: and ye are Christ's and Christ is God's (*eite kosmos, eite Zoe, eite thanatos*).

(k) 1 Cor. 8: 4. We know there is no idol in creation (i.e. no full and true representation of God '*en kosmo(i)*').

(l) 1 Cor. 14: 10. There are, it may be, so many kinds of voices in creation (same Greek).

(m) 2 Cor. 5: 19. God was in Christ reconciling creation to Himself (no article).

(n) Gal. 6: 14. Through which creation has been crucified unto me, and I unto creation (twice, without article).

(o) Eph. 1: 4. Even as He chose us in Him, before foundation of creation (same Greek as (d)).

(p) Phil. 2: 15. Among whom ye are seen as light-bearers in creation (same Greek as (g), (k), (l)).

(q) Col. 2: 20. If ye died with Christ from the rudiments of the world (*apo tōn stoicheiōn tou kosmou*), why, as though living in creation (*zōntes en kosmo(i)*—i.e. in elemental creation not purged by Christ), do ye subject yourselves to ordinances?

(r) Heb. 4: 3; 9: 26. From foundation of creation (the same accepted phrase as above).

(s) 1 Pet. 1: 20. Before foundation of creation (same phrase with *pro*).

(t) 2 Pet. 2: 5. [God] spared not an ancient world, but preserved Noah with seven others . . . when He brought a flood upon a world of ungodly men (*archaiou kosmou . . . kataklusmon kosmo(i) asebōn epaxas*).

(u) Rev. 13: 8; 17: 8. From foundation of creation (usual phrase).

Chapter 14

THE HOMOLOGIA

There was a promise, or perhaps a threat, at the end of Chapter 2 of a later rather dull chapter on the '*homologia*'. The *homologia* is *the confession of faith*, and *homologein* means *to confess the faith*. I think that our mystery-creed was called *the homologia*, at least in Asia Minor, and I will explain why.

In Chapter 2 we traced the connexion in the mind of the author of 1 Timothy (it will save time to call him St. Paul, whose thought is undoubtedly behind the Pastoral epistles) between Timothy's 'good *confession*' (6: 12), our Lord's 'good *confession*' (6: 13), the '*deposit* of the *faith*' (6: 20, 21), the record in the fourth gospel of how our Lord made the 'good *confession*' before Pilate that He had come into the world to witness to the *truth* (John 18: 37), and the taking up of the word *truth* in 1 Timothy 3: 15 with the word *homologoumenōs*, meaning *confessed*-ly or *we confess that* . . .

I will now answer some probable objections:

(1) 'But St. John only makes the witness to truth a secondary part of Jesus' confession before Pilate. Pilate asks Him whether He is a king, and Jesus answers that to this end He was born and to this end He came into the world—that is, to be a king—so that He might witness to truth (the truth of His kingship).'

It sounds like that because the words 'to this end' are repeated (Greek: *eis touto*). But in the recently discovered Ryland's fragment[1]—the earliest fragment of any of the gospels, about A.D. 125—the repetition is not there. We should therefore read as follows:

> Pilate therefore said to him, Art thou a king? Jesus answered, Thou sayest that I am a king—to this end have I been born. And I have come into the world in order that I may bear witness to the truth; everyone who is of the truth heareth my voice. Pilate saith unto him, What is truth?

The whole emphasis is altered by the omission of the second *eis touto*. Jesus is now saying to Pilate, 'Yes, have it your own way—I was born to be king. And my purpose in coming into the world was witness to truth; those who are true recognize me as true.' Pilate said, 'Is there any such thing as truth?'

So when St. Paul has told Timothy that he is writing (in case he gets delayed) to let him know the pattern of Christian behaviour in the household of God—i.e. the Church of the living God, pillar and stay of the truth—his mind turns back naturally to Pilate's 'What is truth?' and Christ's confession of Himself as witness to truth: and so to our confession of Him as truth— the same connexion of thought as in 6: 12 and 13. What more apt moment for a repetition of that confession-pattern which must be the Christian's guide to the truth in Christ? But, since it is to be written, it must be in the veiled language which Christians use in self-defence: first *hŏmŏlŏgoumenōs* which as one word usually means 'by common consent', but which as two words means 'we confess that'; then the title and introduction, and then the verse cryptic to any but a Christian.

(2) 'But if *homologoumenōs* means 'by common consent' it cannot conceivably introduce the creed-formula of a minority sect. The division into two words is pure guesswork by Dr. Badcock; and the particle *hōs* (meaning that) is very seldom used in that meaning in the New Testament.'

That is true; but it is used in that meaning after a verb of 'saying' twice at least. In 2 Timothy 1: 3, St. Paul says: 'I thank God that (*hōs*) . . .', and in Luke 24: 35, 'they explained . . . that he was known to them in the breaking of the bread'.

But even if we dismiss Dr. Badcock's guess that it is *homologoumen hōs* (the H or rough breathing is not written in uncial Greek, or cursive Greek until later times), and read *homologoumenōs*, it could still introduce a formula which is not generally agreed upon. The word is used three times in the fourth book of Maccabees (6: 31; 7: 16; 16: 1) to introduce the formula 'Godly reason (*ho eusebēs logismos*) is master of the passions'. As the whole purpose of 4 Maccabees is declared to be to shew that this formula is true, it obviously cannot be a matter of common consent. 'Godly reason', to the author, meant reasoned adherence to the Jewish law; the formula therefore had something of the nature of a creed. Those are the only three times that the word occurs in the Septuagint; and it never occurs in the New Testament except in our verse.

The date of 4 Maccabees is between A.D. 38 (Caligula) and the destruction of Jerusalem in A.D. 70.[2] It was a book accepted among Christians, and may well have been known to St. Paul[3] (or the author of 1 Timothy). If so the word would readily have come to the lips of a converted Jew,[4] more particularly as the opening words *ho eusebēs logismos* contain the *eusebeia* root (godliness).

From classical Greek, too, we can find a passage in Plato (Symp. 202 B) which uses, not *homologoumenōs* but its verb *homologoumai* in a confessional sense: 'God is confessed by all to be great' (*Homologeitai ge para pantōn megas theos einai*).

(3) 'But surely, even the noun *homologia* and the verb *homologein* often mean other things in the New Testament than confess—in the credal sense?'

The verb is used thirteen times in a credal sense, of faith in Christ:

(i)	Matt. 10: 32 ⎫	Similar sayings—(Luke) Everyone
(ii)	Luke 12: 8 ⎭	who shall *confess* in me before men, in him also shall the Son of Man confess before the angels of God.

This is *confession of the Name*, which means acknowledgment that a person is what he claims to be (cf. Exod. 33: 19; 34: 5 ff.; Deut. 12: 11; Num. 6: 27; John 17: 6, 26; Acts 9: 15; Phil. 2: 9–11). This meaning of Name is not confined to the Bible, but pervades all primitive communities. In our own language 'making a name for oneself' means to justify a man's claim to greatness.[5]

(iii)	John 9: 22	the Jews had already agreed that if any were to *confess* him to be Christ, he should be put out of the synagogue.
(iv)	John 12: 42.	they did not *confess* him.
(v) ⎫	Rom. 10: 8–10.	The word (*rēma*—more like a formula) is very near to you, in your mouth
(vi) ⎭		

and in your heart: this is the word
(*rēma*) of faith (*pistis*) which we proclaim: because if you *confess* with
your mouth 'Jesus is Lord', and believe in your heart that God raised
him from the dead, you will be saved;
for with their heart men put their
trust in goodness, whilst they *confess*
it with their mouth, and so gain salvation.

In (v) and (vi) it is associated with the early brief confession
of faith in Jesus as conqueror.

(vii)	1 Tim. 6: 12.	You *confessed* the good confession.
(viii)	Heb. 13: 15.	the fruit of lips *confessing* in (or 'to', dative) his Name.
{ (ix)	1 John 2: 23.	he who *confesses* the Son has the Father also.
{ (x), (xi)	1 John 4: 2, 3.	Every spirit who *confesses* that Jesus Christ has come in the flesh is from God: and every spirit who does not *confess* Jesus is not from God.
(xii)	1 John 4: 15.	Whoever *confesses* that 'Jesus is the Son of God', God remains in him and he in God.
(xiii)	2 John 7.	they that *confess* not that Jesus Christ cometh in the flesh.

Of the thirteen other times that the verb *homologein* is used in
the New Testament, five have a semi-credal sense, and express
faith but not in Christ.

(i)	Acts 23: 8.	the Pharisees *confessed* belief in a Resurrection.
(ii)	Acts 24: 14.	Paul *confessed* belief in Christianity in general.
(iii)	Titus 1: 16.	the defiled and unbelieving *confess* knowledge of God with their lips, but belie it in their actions.
(iv), (v) and (vi)	Matt. 10: 32 Luke 12: 8 Rev. 3: 5	The Son of Man will *confess* before the angels those who have confessed him (*v. supr.*).

The next three passages have a negative sense in the confession:

(vii)	Matt. 7: 23.	Christ will *confess* that he never knew some who claimed to belong to him.
(viii), (ix) John 1: 20.		John Baptist '*confessed* and denied not; and he *confessed*, I am not the Christ'.

Once the word is used to mean 'admit':

(x)	Heb. 11: 13.	The patriarchs *confessed* themselves to be strangers and pilgrims.

Twice the verb is used to mean 'promise':

(xi)	Matt. 14: 7.	Herod *promised* to Salome whatever she should ask.
(xii)	Acts 7: 17.	God *promised* to Abraham.

Once only is it used to mean confession of sins:

(xiii)	1 John 1: 9.	If we *confess* our sins, He is faithful . . .

The noun *homologia* is used six times in the New Testament, every time to mean a confession of faith in Jesus Christ:

(i)	2 Cor. 9: 13.	glorifying God for the obedience of your *confession* unto the gospel of Christ.
(ii), (iii)	1 Tim. 6: 12, 13.	The 'good *confession*' passages.
(iv)	Heb. 3: 1.	consider the Apostle and High Priest of our *confession*, even Jesus.
(v)	Heb. 4: 14.	Having then a great High Priest who hath passed through the heavens, Jesus the Son of God, let us hold fast our *confession*.
(vi)	Heb. 10: 23.	Let us hold fast the *confession* of our hope, that it waver not; for he is faithful that promised.

So although the verb *homologein* does not always refer to confession of Christ, it has almost always the confessional sense. The noun *homologia* has no other sense at all in the New Testament.

It would therefore be very strange, for that reason alone, if *homologoumenōs* were used without any sense of introducing a confession of Christ.

(4) 'But in the time of the early fathers *confession* was not connected with a true understanding of the faith. Was it not simply a matter of courage, and of being prepared to face persecution?'

It is true that the terms *homologia*, *homologein* and *homologētēs* (confessor) did develop the sense of confession under threat. But that for the most part came later than the period which concerns our creed-form.

For example, Ignatius developed the sense of *homologein* along the lines which we have seen appearing in the Johannine epistles. There already it began to mean confession of a true faith, faith in Jesus as coming in the flesh or as Son of God.

Here is Ignatius (Smyrn. 5): 'How does it profit me if a man praises me but blasphemes my Lord by not *confessing* him as flesh-bearing?'

And in the next section (Smyrn. 6) he develops this sense logically to apply to the Eucharistic elements: 'They stay away from the Eucharist and prayer, because they do not *confess* that the Eucharist is the flesh of our Saviour Christ, which (i.e. the flesh) suffered for our sins, which (i.e. the flesh again) the Father raised in His goodness.'

Here we get an early suggestion of the Eucharist as 'an extension of the Incarnation'—to use an overworked phrase.

Ignatius is not alone in using *homologein* in a doctrinal sense. Here is Polycarp (Ep. Phil. 7):

For everyone who does not *confess* that Jesus has come in the flesh is anti-Christ. And whoever does not *confess* the witness of the Cross is of the devil: and whoever perverts the words of the Lord to his own private purposes, and says that there is no resurrection or no judgment, he is the first-born of Satan.

Here confession clearly means confession not simply of Christ against threat of persecution, but of an orthodox idea of Christ against false ideas. It involves a true understanding of the faith.

Indeed, in section 2 of the same letter Polycarp has already urged Christians to leave behind the empty *mataiologia*, which means a 'vain form of words' and is in contrast with *homologia*, the true form of words. He does not use *homologia*, but instead follows the injunction with an actual creed-form which I shall examine in Chapter 16. It does not follow strictly the pattern of the mystery-creed, but has points in common. In it the glorified Christ, to whom all beings are subject, is the centre as He must always be for man.

This sense of *homologia* continued to be used, though persecution tended to over-emphasize its second meaning as *confession under threat*. In Justin Martyr confession contains both senses:

> Ptolemaeus *confessed* the guidance of the divine virtue . . . a man who denies something either denies it because he condemns the thing itself, or because he thinks himself unworthy of it, or is not in tune with it . . .' and so in denying it 'he runs away from the *confession*' (2nd Apol. P.G. 6, 445, B.C.).

A certain Lucius protested against Ptolemaeus' condemnation, which was not earned by any crime or misdemeanour, but because 'he *confessed* the imputation of the name of Christian'.

In the first Apology Justin has said, 'If anyone *confess* himself (a Christian) you punish him for his *confession*' (333, A, sec. 4). To Trypho the Jew he says: 'We are beheaded and crucified (etc.) . . . because we do not shirk the *confession*' (Dial. Tr., p. 729, sec. 110).

This confession of the Name of Christ at great cost gave it also its great power. For instance, the pseudo-Ignatius (3rd or 4th cent.) wrote to the Philippians (sec. 3) about the *power* of the confession of the Cross: 'The prince of this world rejoices whenever anyone denies the Cross: for he knows that *confession* of the Cross is his destruction. For this is the sign which stands over against his power: when he sees it he shudders: when he hears of it he is afraid.'

The confession has become the sacrifice which it involves: it is a 'trophy', in the technical sense, with the arms of the conquered nailed to it.

Confessors have become almost an order of the ministry. In his letter to the Antiochenes, pseudo-Ignatius sends greetings to sub-deacons, readers, singers, door-keepers, sextons, exorcists and *confessors*.

We are all familiar with the situation which developed, and the power which confessors came to possess. Bishops in all parts, and especially in North Africa, were faced with this difficulty. Clement of Alexandria devotes a whole chapter of his Miscellanies to the question (IV, 9, P.G. 8, pp. 1279–86): he insists that the courageous act of 'confession' is not in itself a true confession, unless it comes from one who has tried to live according to the pattern of Christ in his life. In fact *eusebeia* (godliness) is the outward expression of the mystery-creed.

But in Egypt, long before the end of persecution, Dionysius, Bishop of Alexandria, had written of the '. . . holy washing, and the faith and *confession* which comes before it', bringing together *pistis* (faith) and *homologia* (confession) in quite the old way. Athanasius did the same in his letter to the emperor Jovian, when he referred to the creed of Nicaea as the *faith (pistis) confessed* by the fathers at Nicaea. So also Cyril of Alexandria spoke of the confession of an orthodox belief in the baptism which saves us. In the Der-Balyzeh papyrus (6th or 7th century, but with early material) we find: '. . . the newly-enlightened *confesses* the *faith* . . . I believe in God the Father Almighty and in His only begotten Son our Lord Jesus Christ and in the Holy Ghost and in resurrection of flesh in the Holy Catholic Church.'[6]

This is a full confession of faith, and the mystery-creed has become Trinitarian: but the flesh-spirit emphasis is there—

Spirit	*Flesh*
1. God, Father, Almighty,———→	2. Only begotten Son,
3. Our Lord,	4. Jesus Christ,
5. The Holy Ghost,	6. Resurrection of flesh in the universal Church.

NOTES

[1] An unpublished fragment of the 4th Gospel in the John Rylands library. C. H. Roberts; Manch. Univ. Press, 1935.

[2] R. H. Charles, *Apocrypha and Pseudepigrapha of the Old Testament*, vol. II, p. 653 ff.

[3] F. H. Badcock, *The Pauline Epistles*, pp. 115–33. If he does not prove his case, he shews at least what a treacherous witness vocabulary may be.

[4] There is a link between the Pastorals and 4 Maccabees; see Moffatt,

Introduction to the Literature of the New Testament, pp. 414–15. Also see J.T.S., New Series, vol. II, p. 167, note by R. Leaney.

[5] A. H. McNeile, Westminster Commentary on Exod. 33: 19. See *A Theological Word Book of the Bible* on 'Name', p. 157.

[6] See Dion. Alex. in Euseb. H.E. VII, 8. P.G. 26, p. 813, 1 c—on Athanasius. Justin adv. Orig. P.G. 86, p. 967 on Cyril. Also *An Early Euchologium* by C. H. Roberts and Dom B. Capelle; 1949, Louvain.

Chapter 15

THE GROWTH OF A CREED

RUFINUS has a story of how the Apostles' Creed sprang from twelve spirit-guided utterances of the Twelve, after the Ascension. I do not claim that even for our *homologia* (it will be convenient if I may now call our mystery-creed by its Greek name). This extraordinarily compact summary of essential belief was no immediate growth. Some of its teaching, e.g. its universalism, was not realized at all until Peter's vision and visit to Cornelius, and not fully sanctioned until after the Council of Jerusalem in Acts 15. The other themes were still seen as in a glass, darkly. But its growth must have kept step with the writing of the books of the New Testament, though it may have reached its present form before any of the gospels or the Acts reached their final form. None the less, we should be able to trace its growing pattern in the early sections of the 'Preaching and Teaching' which lie behind gospels and Acts and epistles.

The date and authorship of the Pastoral epistles is still a matter for debate. Fortunately it does not matter greatly. The *homologia* is a quotation of a well-established formula. My own view is that after the fall of Jerusalem, when the preaching of St. Paul was coming into its own without Jewish-Christian rivalry, his liturgical and pastoral instructions were much in demand. A single editor gathered together scraps of letters or even oral instructions given mainly to Timothy and Titus—the whole being influenced by the editor's style and vocabulary, and his sense of the needs of the time. The material and tone I believe to be Pauline. But the pattern of the *homologia* was, I believe, established at least by A.D. 60. This date rests upon the Gospel of St. Mark which shews the pattern more clearly than any other New Testament book, as we shall see. But I must begin at the beginning.

A. The Petrine Speeches in the Acts

Professor Torrey has argued, in *The Composition and Date of Acts*, that the author of Acts used a continuous Aramaic document for Chapters 1 15: 35. Professors C. H. Dodd and T. W. Manson support much of his argument, without necessarily accepting it all.

In 1949, Professor H. F. D. Sparkes read a paper on 'The Semitisms of the Acts' to the Oxford Society of Historical Theology (see their abstract of proceedings 1948–9, pp. 53 ff.). In this he argued strongly against Torrey's thesis; and these are his main points:

(1) Torrey suggests that '*epi to auto*' is a mistranslation of an Aramaic word of the Judaean dialect, which means not 'together' but 'greatly' (Acts 2: 47). Sparkes argues that in the four other places in the first five chapters in which the phrase occurs, the meaning 'greatly' is unsuitable. But it does not follow that in the other four places St. Luke was translating the same Aramaic word: it is probable, perhaps, but not certain: translators do not always translate the same word by the same word. In septuagintal Greek, *epi to auto* has become a single word meaning 'together': it is often written as such.

(2) His second point is a convincing one. St. Luke uses the Septuagint for his quotations from the Old Testament in Acts, and the background of his writing is the Septuagint. But an Aramaic original would use quotations from the Hebrew: he quotes Dr. Lowther Clark on 'The Use of the Septuagint in Acts', in *The Beginnings of Christianity*, vol. II. If St. Luke imitated the Septuagint, the case for Aramaisms is weakened, because what could be Aramaisms could also be septuagintal Greek. 'James', he remarks, 'in Chapter 15 quotes Amos from the Septuagint, which was necessary to his point.' Convincing though this is, it is at least possible that a Greek writer, belonging to a Church which usually used the Septuagint version, should have altered quotations, even in an Aramaic original, to the accepted text which the Church used.[1] And even James, a Hebrew of Hebrews, was also a Galilaean; and the Septuagint was very commonly used in Galilee.

(3) Dr. Sparkes then shews evidence of Aramaisms in the second half of the Acts, which 'set the problem in an entirely fresh light'. But an artist would naturally tend to continue in the same style as he had begun.

I think that Dr. Sparkes is right, if a man who is no Aramaic scholar may presume to express a judgment between two men who are Aramaists. That is to say, I think it is unlikely that St. Luke used a written Aramaic source. Even after reading Professor Torrey, the written source theory is not convincing. But it seems very likely that St. Luke made use of much evidence given to him in Aramaic, including perhaps the accounts of the speeches. There may be septuagintalisms in St. Luke, but neither in Gospel nor in Acts did St. Luke write septuagintal Greek: on the other hand, he would be nearest to doing so when he was rendering into Greek what he had received in Aramaic. Even Dr. Sparkes admits the possibility of this: 'Some semitisms are attributable directly to his Aramaic speaking informants: some, too, to the unconscious influence upon him of the Semitic Greek patois current among so many of his co-religionists:' 'but,' he adds, 'most, I believe are his own "septuagintalisms".'

The fashion for multiplying written sources is fortunately passing. Those who have lived and worked among races who have no written language will know how phenomenal their memory can be. A story can be told and retold time after time with no word altered. Those of us who deal much with children, and who tell and retell the same stories, know that children allow no alterations or omissions: and under such surveillance, we sometimes surprise ourselves with the accuracy of our own memories.

I would therefore expect an account of Peter's speeches, given to St. Luke many years later, to be accurate in order and emphasis, if not always in phraseology. The account of the speech at Cornelius's house, both recent and local (if St. Luke was the author of the Acts), would be particularly accurate, though it is difficult to see why it should have been given in Aramaic: perhaps it was given in a Greek which was full of semitisms, which were faithfully reproduced; the evidence of Aramaism is there at its strongest.

I

The speeches as we have them, then, may well be examples of the primitive preaching. If so their value as evidence is not a static value. It should be possible to see in them a development of the pattern of the preaching, containing within it the seeds of the *homologia* doctrine and its two-element arrangement. The pattern does not appear in perspective at first. Whether the speeches are early and genuine, or late and Thucydidean, we can only expect traces of the pattern. If St. Luke invented the speeches, what there was of the pattern would be static in them: but if the speeches were based on genuine recollections of men who heard them, the traces would be faint at first, but growing clearer in the later speeches.

It was impossible to avoid tabulation, and the table is as clear as it could be made: it shews the gradual emergence of a pattern of preaching.

The Homologia Pattern and its Development in the Petrine Speeches
(1) *Acts 2: 14–36.*
Introduction: prophecies fulfilled.

{ 22. Jesus of Nazareth { 23. sent to judgment, killed, (Manifested in flesh)	22. Designated by God, signs given, 24. God freed Him from death. . . . 32. . . . and raised Him. (Justified in spirit)
32. 'We are witnesses'. 33. . . . He hath poured forth this which ye see and hear. 34. David did not ascend, but confessed belief. (Believed on)	33. By the right hand of God exalted and having received the promise of the Holy Ghost, 36. Let all Israel know that God has made Jesus Lord and Christ. (Received up in glory)

The first and last pairs of the *homologia* are paralleled in substance, but vaguely.
(2) *Acts 2: 38–9.* A practical instruction.

38. Repent and be baptized in the Name of Jesus Christ unto remission of sins, (Visible manifestation)	38. and ye shall receive the gift of the Holy Ghost. (Justification in the spirit)

39. To you is the promise, (Grounds for belief and hope)

39. and to all that are afar off, as many as the Lord our God shall call upon Him. (A hint of the proclamation among nations)

Only a vague suggestion of a flesh-spirit pattern.

(3) *Acts 3: 13–21.*

God glorified—

13. —His servant Jesus, betrayed, denied, (Manifested in flesh)

13. The Holy and righteous One. (Justified in spirit)

14f. You asked for a taker of life, killed the Prince of life, (Death)

15. Whom God raised from the dead. (Resurrection)

15. 'We are witnesses'.

Parenthesis, vv. 16–18.

19. Repent and be forgiven, (exorcism on earth)
so there may come seasons of refreshing.
20. And that He may send the Christ, even Jesus: (The redemption of creation, and hope of Parousia)

19. that your sins may be blotted out, (Justification in heaven)
from the presence of the Lord;
21. whom the heaven must receive until the times of restoration. (Received up in glory, though yet incomplete)

(4) *Acts 4: 10–12.*

Be it known to you all—

10. Jesus of Nazareth whom you crucified, (Manifested in flesh) in Him is this man whole. (Sign of power; i.e. Christ in control of powers of evil)

10. whom God raised up, (Justified in spirit)

11. The stone rejected by you—

11. —made head of the corner.

12. No salvation on earth by other means: (Believed on in creation)	12. neither is there any other name under heaven wherein is salvation. (Subjection of heavenly powers: this is something between proclaimed among nations' and 're-ceived up in glory'.)

A slightly clearer pattern.

(5) *Acts 5: 29–32*. An inverted pattern. (Very slight evidence, if any, of Aramaism).

Spirit	*Flesh*
29. We must obey God,	29. —rather than men.
30. God raised Jesus (Justified in spirit)	30. —whom you crucified. (Manifested in flesh)
31. God exalted Him (Received up in glory)	31. —to give repentance to Israel, and forgiveness. (Exorcism on earth) 'We are witnesses'
32. The Holy Ghost is also witness, (Justified in spirit)	32. —whom God has given to them that obey Him. (Believed on in creation)

The inverted pattern and its confusion is perhaps due to con-siderable editing, or poor memories.

(6) *Acts 10: 36–43*. The Cornelius speech.

Introduction: All in every nation are now shewn to be ac-ceptable to God: I therefore proclaim to you the word (*rēma*) which God sent to the children of Israel (Proclaimed among nations).

36. Peace through Jesus Christ (Parenthesis)	36. He is Lord of all.
38. Jesus of Nazareth, (Manifested in flesh)	38. God anointed Him with the Holy Ghost and with power. (Justified in spirit)

38. He overthrew the tyranny   38. For God was with Him.
    of the devil;
    (Seen of angels)
39. Whom they crucified   40. —but God raised up.

(Death-resurrection doublet of first pair)

41. 'We are witnesses'.
42. He charged us to preach   42. —Judge of quick and
    and bear witness that God   dead.
    has appointed Him—   (Received up in glory)
    (Believed on in creation)

43. The prophets bear witness   43. —will receive forgiveness.
    that believers on His Name   (Christ as Lord)
    —

(Believed on in creation)

This pattern is well on the way to the *homologia*. When the new and startling doctrine, 'Proclaimed among nations', has been digested, it can take its place (which St. Paul's theology gave it—Eph. 3: 1–12) over against the overthrow of the evil powers, i.e. 'seen of angels'. The phrase set against it in this pattern, 'For God was with him,' has really been said already, in the anointing with the Holy Ghost and with power.

B. The Pauline Epistles

In *The Apostolic Preaching and its Developments* Professor Dodd has given us a work the importance of which can hardly be exaggerated. On page 17 he has sifted out the elements of the preaching of the early Church, in the time of the apostles, including an outline of the kerygma of St. Paul, For our purpose we may rearrange it as follows:

Outward-and-visible
(1) Manifested in flesh, prophecy fulfilled, born of the seed of David, died, and was buried,
(3) to deliver us from the present evil age;
(seen of angels)

Inward-and-spiritual
(2) Justified in spirit, new age inaugurated by the coming of Christ, who rose on the third day,

(5) He will come again
(believed on in creation);

(6) He is exalted at the right
hand of God, as Lord
(received up in glory).

Professor Dodd has omitted an important part of the Pauline *kerygma* to match the omission in the *homologia* pattern above. No one can read St. Paul without being struck with the importance to him of 'the principalities and powers in heavenly places'. The *locus classicus* is Ephesians 3: 1–12, which unmistakably links them with the preaching to the nations (the Gentiles).

There are those who deny that St. Paul wrote this epistle, with whom I cannot agree: but at least it reflects Pauline theology in this as in other points. The spirits of the nations—angelic Guardians—are now to be converted through the Church and its missionary work in the apostles: in this Ephesians 3: 1–12 is a commentary on 1 Corinthians 4: 9. And the corroboration is in the epistle to the Colossians, where in chapter 1 St. Paul links up the creation of things in heaven and earth, visible and invisible, 'whether thrones or dominions or principalities or powers', with their reconciliation in Christ through the reconciling of the Gentiles who were alienated and enemies in time past: the Colossians are not to be moved away from the hope of the gospel which was preached 'in all creation under heaven': this is the 'mystery among the nations, which is Christ in you, the hope of glory'.

'Proclaimed among nations' must certainly be added, then, to the outline given by Professor Dodd, who indeed remarks that the *kerygma* as adopted by Paul 'almost certainly did contain more than this'. And the 'nations' are not only the people who make them up on earth, but the spirits who represent them in heaven.

In the Pauline pattern the manifestation in flesh includes the whole ministry, death and burial. Justification in spirit means the resurrection.

The deliverance from the present evil age, has, in all the early teaching, the idea behind it of angelic rulers dispensing the law (Acts 7: 53; Gal. 3: 19; Heb. 2: 2 and 5). Their rule is divinely commissioned, but they have exceeded their powers, or at least outstayed their appointed time.

The promise of the second coming is properly placed in the category 'Believed on in creation'—that same creation which groans and travails in pain, waiting for the 'redemption of the body' (Rom. 8: 22 f.); and whose faith is 'the assurance of things hoped for', which phrase, from the Epistle to the Hebrews (11: 1), is the expression of an idea common to that author, St. Paul (Rom. 8: 24; 2 Cor. 4: 18 and 5: 7) and St. Peter (1 Pet. 1: 8). It is the idea which lies behind this fifth clause of the *homologia*, and points forward to the sixth.

In the eighth chapter of the Epistle to the Romans, after a long 'two-element' discussion which has lasted for three chapters, on law and grace, sin and justification, death and life, flesh and spirit, Paul suddenly breaks into one of his finest poetical passages in verses 38 and 39. Unconsciously perhaps in his rush of feeling, he follows the *homologia* pattern:

(1) neither death, (flesh)

(2) nor life, (spirit)

(3) nor angels, (angels)

(4) nor principalities, (nations)

(5) nor things present, nor things to come, nor powers, nor height, nor depth, nor any other creature, shall be able to separate us from—(creation)

(6) —the love of God which is in Christ Jesus *our Lord.* (glory)

Even the elements which compose the mystery may be looked upon as barriers, if they are objectified or worshipped in themselves—even life itself, as is witnessed by the pathetic pursuit of it in the perpetual motion and change demanded by men and women of to-day.

The pattern is recurrent in the epistles of St. Paul, not always in its completeness, but always shewing its two-element character in the apparent antipathy of flesh and spirit. Passages worth referring to are Romans 1: 1–7; 2 Corinthians 10: 3–5 for (1), (2) and (3), then verses 14–16 for (4), (5) and (6); Ephesians 3: 1–12; Philippians 2: 5–11; 2 Timothy 2: 12.

C. 1 PETER

The first Epistle of St. Peter gives one of the most exact parallels with the *homologia*, as Dr. Selwyn has pointed out (*The First*

Epistle of St. Peter, p. 325 ff.). I would, however, add one point: he is convinced that the 'preaching to the spirits in prison' is the proclamation to the angels of the fall (op. cit., p. 198); but these same angels were the spirits of the nations, divinely commissioned; the preaching to them is thus a direct parallel with 'proclaimed among nations' which appears on the 'spirit' side of the pattern. Peter's line of thought is slightly different from that of the *homologia*. The *homologia* sees Jesus in the flesh conquering spirits of disobedience, and finally through death and conquest receiving the submission of the Guardians of the nations; He is thus proclaimed to the nations (i.e. the departed souls which make them up) in Hades. St. Peter sees the proclamation made as Christ enters the domains of death, 'quickened in spirit'; the proclamation is at once made to the departed of the nations and their Guardians together: as a result God brings all their angels, authorities and powers into subjection to Christ. A glance at the table will make it clear. It is not a chronological business: it is a sequence of thought. Are the Guardians reached through the nations whom they guard? Or are the nations reached by virtue of conquest of their Guardians (A modern parochial and parallel question: are we to approach parents through children, or children through their parents?)

1 Tim. 3: 16.	1 Peter 3: 18–22
(1) Manifested in flesh,	Put to death in flesh,
(2) Justified in spirit,	Quickened in spirit
(3) Seen of angels,	in right of which also (*vide infra*)
(4) Proclaimed among nations,	He went and proclaimed to the spirits in prison;
(5) Believed on in creation,	Baptism now saves you,[2] the answer of a good conscience to God,
(6) Received up in glory.	through resurrection of Jesus Christ, who is on God's right hand, having entered heaven,
	(3) angels and authorities and powers being made subject unto him.

D. The Epistle to the Hebrews[3]

This opens with a creed form, which shews an inverted two-element pattern. The Alexandrines were very much *sui generis*; and though there are parallels with the *homologia* they are not significant. Alexandria was orthodox but different.

E. The Revelation

In Chapter 1 (5–8) there is a good creed-form, with all the clauses of the *homologia* represented, but in a chiasmic pattern with the second pair inverted. It is a Christ-creed and a two-element creed.

(1) (Manifested in flesh) 'Jesus Christ, the faithful witness.'

(2) (Justified in spirit) 'The first-born of the dead'.

(4) (Proclaimed among national Guardians, who submitted) 'Ruler of the "kings" of the earth'.

(3) (Seen of angels—i.e. exorcism of evil) 'Loves us, and loosed us from our sins in his blood'.

(5) (Believed on in creation—our hope and security) 'Made us a Kingdom, priests to God and his Father'.

(6) (Received up in glory) 'To him be glory . . .'.

The closeness of the reference in (4) will be seen by a glance at Psalm 2. 'Kings of the earth' are more than earthly rulers: earthly rulers should symbolize the spirit of the nation, but the spirit itself is the angelic guardian. Psalm 2 was a much quoted one in the early Church.

F. The Gospel of St. Mark

St. Mark's Gospel may be compared with a symphony which combines folk melodies with the musical idiom of its own age, but has its own purpose and inspiration.

That purpose is sufficiently stated in the first seven (Greek) words: 'The beginning of the gospel of Jesus Christ, the Son of God.' Whether the words 'the Son of God' belong to the original text or not, they shew clearly what St. Mark set out to do.

The obvious general pattern is:

(A) Chapters 1–9: 8. Public preaching, with signs of the kingdom, leading up to the Transfiguration.

(B) Chapters 9: 9–10: 45. Warnings of Passion-Resurrection, and other two-element units of teaching.

Chapters 10: 46–12. The Son of David enters His city.

Chapter 13. The new Deuteronomy.

Chapters 14–16: 8. Passion-Resurrection.

Whilst (B) follows a chronological pattern, the chronology of (A) is less apparent. But there is a pattern, and a familiar one:

(1) 1: 1. Manifested in flesh.

(2) 1: 2–12. Justified in spirit (Baptism, temptation).

(3) 1: 13, 23–7, 34, 39; 3: 11 f., 15; 4: 37–41; 5: 1–20; 4: 7, 13; (Seen of Angels) Ministry of angels after temptation: Recognition by and authority over demons: Control of elements: indeed all healing and other miracles, including the restoration of life, probably come under this head; in them Jesus exercised control over the Powers.

(4) 7: 24–8: 9 (Proclaimed among nations). The Gentile section of the gospel, the Syrophoenician woman, Ephphatha, the feeding of the 4,000 (symbolizing the evangelizing of the Gentiles).[4]

(5) 8: 29 (Believed on in creation). Peter's confession; but this is only the climax: there is continual emphasis on the saving power of faith, without which even Christ could do no mighty work.

(6) 9: 2–8 (Received up in glory). Transfiguration.

This is no complicated working out of motifs: it is the main theme: it is *the* rhythm of the gospel, and its pattern is unmistakable. St. Mark did not write in that pattern because he knew the *homologia*: nor did the *homologia* take St. Mark's pattern to itself. It is the pattern of the Christ, the mystery of godliness. In these chapters it is an anticipated pattern—in terms of time: but it is beyond time: it is the pattern of the pulsation[5] of a fallen creation, reaching out towards God. It is the framework into which the Church is built, and it is significant that it reappears in the appendix to St. Mark's Gospel:

(1) and (2) 16: 9–14. The appearances—manifested in flesh: justified in spirit.

(3) and (4) 16: 17. The signs: casting out devils=seen of angels; speaking with new tongues=proclaimed among nations (also v. 15, 'Go ye into all the world').

(5) 16: 18. The fruits of faith: power to absorb evil things without harm—serpents, deadly things: power to heal. Believed on in creation.

(6) 16: 19. Received up in glory.[6]

G. St. Matthew and St. Luke

St. Matthew follows the pattern of St. Mark, with an explicit reference to *Galilee of the nations* from Isaiah (Matt. 4: 15; Isa. 9: 1). This is a foreshadowing, and not an actual proclamation among nations yet: there is the specific injunction in Chapter 10: 5, 'Go not into any way of the Gentiles, and enter not into any city of the Samaritans.' The time had not yet come. But this is accompanied by the prophecy: '. . . before governors and kings shall ye be brought for my sake, *for a testimony to them and to the Gentiles*' (10: 18). Similarly, the sign of Jonah the prophet is more than a prophecy of the death and resurrection: after 'three days and three nights in the belly of the whale' (12: 40 f.) —that is, after death and resurrection—Jonah travelled to Nineveh and there proclaimed the word of God. This foreshadows the proclamation of the gospel to the nations after the Resurrection. 'After I am raised up, I will go before you into Galilee' (26: 32). The Ninevites (the nations) who listened to and obeyed the word of God from Jonah, will judge the Jews who refused to listen to Christ.

St. Luke makes it clear in his introduction that he means to get events in their right time sequence. All the elements of the *homologia* pattern are there; but he is chiefly concerned to shew how the historical gospel was 'preached unto all nations, beginning from Jerusalem'. He was a Greek; and though as fond of angels and unusual events as anyone, he was more of an historian than philosopher or theologian.

H. The Fourth Gospel

This shews the same pattern, though not in direct sequence. Each couplet is by itself, and leads on to, or arises out of the one after or before it:

(1) 1: 1–18. The prologue: manifested in flesh.

(2) 1: 29–34. The baptism: Justified in spirit. Followed by a

hint of (3) in 1: 51, the saying to Nathanael about angels
ascending and descending upon the Son of Man.

(3) 12: 28–31. The voice from heaven: the people say, 'An
angel spake to him': Jesus says, 'Now is the judgment of this
world: now shall the prince of this world be cast out.'[7] Seen of
angels. There is a hint of (2) in the voice from heaven, which
recalls the baptism (though John does not mention the justify-
ing voice at the baptism). We may even go further back and see
a hint of (1) in the palm procession—the true King of Israel
shewn coming 'in the Name'.

(4) 12: 20–4. The acceptance of the Gentiles: followed by
verses 37–40, the accompanying rejection of the Jews. Proclaimed among nations. It is to be noticed that (3) has become
sandwiched between the two halves of (4): but the two ideas are
inseparably linked. Verses 42 and 43 are clear foreshadowings
of (5) and (6): the belief of the rulers, but not yet full belief;
their love of glory, but not the true glory.

(5) 19, 38–20: 31. Believed on in creation. From Chapter 18:
37 onwards, the actors in the Passion story are demonstrating
the nature of their attitude to truth. First Jesus Himself witnesses the good confession, and proclaims the purpose of His
life—to witness to truth. 'Everyone that is of the truth heareth
my voice.' Pilate promptly proclaims his agnosticism. 'The
Jews' proclaim their faith in worldly heroism: 'Not this man but
Barabbas,' and Barabbas, observes John, was a robber: force is
the sanction of the world's faith. The contrast between Caesar's
kingship and that of the Christ is then made clear: Caesar has
power (19: 10, 11), real power and given from above, which is
mixed up with sin: the Christ has a crown of thorns and complete innocence, and is acknowledged king by Caesar (v. 14).
The chief priests then make their confession of faith: 'We have
no king but Caesar.' There follows a hint of (4), the proclamation among the nations: Jesus of Nazareth is given His title,
which is written in Hebrew, Latin and Greek—the language of
the chosen people, and the languages of the two halves of the
Gentile world—and this title is not to be withdrawn: it is Caesar's confession of the truth, and at the same time an admission
of his helplessness. Two of the rulers who had shewn imperfect
belief before, Joseph and Nicodemus, then shew their true

belief in their actions, in verses 38 to 41. In Chapter 20: 8, the beloved disciple sees and believes: his faith is the beginning; Mary Magdalene follows; then the other apostles without Thomas, who later makes his full and true confession of faith (v. 28). The whole purpose of the fourth gospel is finally proclaimed to be 'that we may believe' without having seen.

(6) *20: 17, 31.* 'I am not yet ascended,' said the risen Christ to Mary Magdalene, but 'I am ascending'. In English idiom, and sometimes in Greek, this may mean 'I am just on the point of ascending': various scholars have suggested that it means 'I shall be ascending this afternoon', and assume that the Ascension took place on Easter Day. Such a view only needs to be stated baldly, as I have just done, for us to see how utterly out of tune it is with the Resurrection story. *Anabaino* (Greek) means exactly what it says, 'I am ascending.' Jesus had said that there were 'many mansions', i.e. resting places, and that He was going to prepare for His disciples to follow. I have tried to shew in Chapter 12 that the ascent from earth to heaven, from man to God, answers to the second forty years in the wilderness—the forty years which ended in the promised land: it is symbolized in the forty days between Easter and Ascension. The end is Christ, the Son of God—and, for us, life in His Name. And *a Name* means Glory. Received up in glory.

It may be objected that in any gospel it will be possible to find these elements, and that the discovery of them proves no special pattern. If that is said, I think what is really meant is that the discovery of the elements in a certain order does not prove that the evangelist deliberately set them out in that order to fit the *homologia* or anything else: and with that I hasten to agree. If the *homologia* is the summary of the pattern of the truth, the same pattern will be found in all who tell the truth about Christ: the less deliberate the arrangement, the more impressive the argument for it as a pattern of truth.

I will recapitulate. The two parts of the first couplet are complementary, Incarnation and Baptism. The reference to angels in 1: 51, is only a promise of (3) 'Seen of angels'. Two passages may be pointers to the proclamation of Him among nations: the receiving of Him by the Galilaeans in 4: 43 f., and His own words in 10: 16: but the real thing only happens when

Philip and Andrew bring the Greeks to Jesus (12: 20 ff.), who accepts this as a sign that His hour has come. It is not necessary to assume that the Greeks were Grecian Jews. The voice from heaven then proclaimed judgment on this world and the expulsion of its tyrant prince in the eternal present. This idea can be expressed in terms relevant to any particular age: the only important thing about the terms is that they shall be relevant: to Christ it was the rejection of the kingdoms of this world and the glory of them; to the early Church it was the conquest and control of rebellious guardian angels of the nations; to us it is the riddance from a spirit of nationalism which has become demonic. But whatever the terms, the idea underlying 'Seen of angels, proclaimed among nations' is fundamental to the gospel. The gospel's original ending is on the firm note of the last couplet. Glory to him who is believed on, and through him to those who believe on Him. The appendix, Chapter 21, underlines the universal scope of the gospel, and the responsibility of the shepherds of the other sheep, not of the Jewish fold.

If St. Mark shews the clearest pattern, the fourth gospel is the exposition of it and therefore even more significant: it underlines the true emphases, and leads from one to the other.

I have insisted that the *homologia* pattern is in balanced couplets—and so indeed it is. But the clauses are also thesis, antithesis and synthesis. 'Manifested in flesh—justified in spirit', and therefore 'seen of angels'. 'Justified in spirit—seen of angels', and therefore 'proclaimed among nations'. 'Seen of angels—proclaimed among nations', and therefore 'believed on in creation'. 'Proclaimed among nations—believed on in creation', and therefore 'received up in glory'. It is more than a creed. It is food for profound meditation, and meditation of a kind which has been forgotten.

NOTES

[1] The Septuagint was considered the authoritative text by the early Church. When Justin Martyr was disputing with Trypho the Jew, Trypho quoted Deut. 32: 8, from the Hebrew; but Justin corrected him with the Septuagint version, which supports the commission given by God to angels over the nations. See Dial. Tr., 131.

[2] See E. G. Selwyn, *The First Epistle of St. Peter*, p. 205 f. The 'answer' is

in Greek *ĕpĕrōtēma*, which in Latin is translated *stipulatio*: this was the clause in a contract 'containing the formal question, and consent (*homologia*) of the contracting parties'. It is therefore a natural term to use of the Christian *homologia*, which was given as the Christian response in baptism.

[3] For convenience I have taken the Gospels together, and therefore have taken Hebrews and the Apocalypse first. I am not suggesting that they were written before St. Mark, though it is possible.

[4] See *A Study in St. Mark*, Dr. A. M. Farrer, p. 297 ff.

[5] This is not simply a purple patch. Pulsation is the outward rhythm of a quite inexplicable inward life.

[6] Dr. W. Lock, in his *Pastoral Epistles*, I.C.C., p. 45, notes that Resch *Paulinismus*, p. 397) has noticed the influence of the *homologia* upon Mark 16: 9-19.

[7] But some said that it thundered. It is tempting to associate this with the lightning flash, which our Lord saw as the fall of Satan from heaven in Luke 10: 18.

Chapter 16

THE PASSING OF A CREED

WE may begin with Ignatius. His letters are full of references to the flesh-and-spirit pattern of the Christian faith: he refuses to let the two become separated either in his Christology or in his Eucharistic teaching. His letter to the Smyrnaeans begins with something very like an exposition of the *homologia* pattern (secs. I–VI). Sections I–III could well be dealing with the first couplet, in his insistence (against the Docetists) upon the flesh, and the spiritual reality of the resurrection; the risen Christ was no bodiless daemon.

Section IV contains a curious play on the 'wild beasts': they are real wild beasts who are going to devour Ignatius, yet they are wild beasts in human form (devil-possessed?) and also wild beasts to be with whom is to be in company with God: this section may well reflect ideas which we have found connected with the second couplet (*v.* Chapter 9, *supra*).

Section V is concerned with those who refuse to believe, whom He refuses even to remember, 'until they repent and return to the passion which is our resurrection'.

The first two sentences of section VI concern the judgment which awaits even the powers of heaven, if they refuse to believe 'in the blood of Christ (who is God)'. The 'blood' is the spirit side of the sacrament of the Eucharist, and the Life which is won through the death of the body. Belief in the blood is then the acceptance of a sacrifice which is an atonement for the Powers of heaven as well as for men.

Sections V and VI are therefore negative versions of the last couplet of the *homologia*: 'Believed on in creation'—those who do not believe will be rejected, or, if angels, will be judged—the implication being that the submission of the Powers will usher in the final glory. 'He that receiveth, let him receive': receive what? What does an initiate receive, if not an exposition of the faith which he is to confess? Lest there should be any doubt that *the faith* is what he has been expounding, he adds that 'faith and love (*agape*) are all in all': Christians are to beware of those who hold strange doctrine; they shew their lack of love by their lack of care for widow, orphan, afflicted, prisoner, hungry or thirsty; they shew their lack of faith by failing to see the flesh-and-spirit pattern in the Eucharist. Finally in section XII, Ignatius salutes the whole ministry 'in the *name* of Jesus Christ, and in His flesh and blood, in His passion and resurrection, which was both carnal and spiritual'—three flesh-and-spirit pairs qualifying 'the name'.

The two-element rhythm may again be seen in the epistle to the Trallians (VIII and IX), in a passage which Professor Cullmann himself connects with the *homologia*:[1] 'Arm yourselves with gentleness, and regain yourselves *in faith* which is *flesh of the Lord*, and *in love*, which is *blood of Jesus Christ*.'

Not very much like a form of confession, it may be thought: but we are not looking for the *homologia* itself, but indications of its pattern behind phrases and suggestions. Here we have an indication, and a very clear one, that Ignatius knew of, and was reminding his readers of, a form of *faith* which was the outward-and-visible sign of Christ in them, *flesh of the Lord* he calls it: this must be reinforced by the inward-and-spiritual grace, namely *love* which is the sign of the Spirit, *blood of Jesus Christ* he calls it. It shews that the flesh and spirit pattern was of the *esse* of the Christian life: to make the sacramental nature of it beyond question, he chooses his illustrations from the Eucharist—the heart of Christian sacramentalism.

Note the chiasmic pattern which is deliberate: 'blood' in the religious sense is 'life', and so is on the spirit side of the pattern:

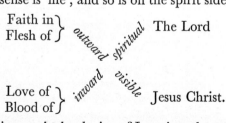

Faith in / Flesh of } *outward* *spiritual* The Lord

Love of / Blood of } *inward* *visible* Jesus Christ.

The chiasmus is the device of Ignatius: the two-element pattern is that of the *homologia*. This reference to the *homologia* is

K

introduced by his saying that he keeps watch over them, because he foresees the snares of the devil: it is followed, in section IX, after a short historical type of Christ-creed, with the statement of the witness of celestial, terrestrial and infernal powers: '. . . he was truly crucified and died, in the sight of beings in heaven, on earth, and under the earth.' And after the chiasmus (VIII) he adds, 'Give no occasion to the nations, lest by reason of a few fools the many godly be blasphemed.'[2]

He has referred to all the clauses of the *homologia*: the flesh is justified in the spirit of Jesus who is Lord and Christ: faith in the Lord is realized in the sacrificial love of Jesus Christ; we see in Him a God in whom we can believe, and trust. All are witnesses to this manifestation of God-in-man, angels, men and devils: it was seen of angels—proclaimed among nations.

Polycarp's *homologia*, written out but not named in opposition to the 'empty mataiologia' (Phil. II) contains death and resurrection (manifested—justified), ascension and session (received up), subjection of all things in heaven and earth (seen of angels —proclaimed), and the service of every living creature (believed on). He adds judgment and final vindication by God, which are implied in the six clauses of the *homologia*. This again is a chiasmic pattern: death (flesh)—resurrection (spirit)—ascension (spirit)—subjection of creation (flesh)—allegiance of creatures (flesh)—judgment and final vindication by God (spirit).

Something approaching the *homologia* pattern appears, perhaps not accidentally, in the same letter (sec. V), when Polycarp says that deacons are to walk 'according to *the truth of the Lord,* who became minister of all':

If we please Him in this age, (i.e. manifest Him in flesh)	we shall receive the age to come. (i.e. we shall be justified in spirit)
As He promised us	to raise us from the dead,
If we behave well, and if we believe	'we shall reign with Him' (received up in glory).
(believed on in creation)	

The actual quotation is from 2 Timothy 2: 12—the faithful saying which is also a balanced two-element credal hymn, but less enlightening as a pattern of doctrine than the *homologia*.

Polycarp is applying the pattern of the mystery to deacons, for whom the two central clauses were not particularly relevant—'seen of angels—proclaimed among nations'.

I have quoted four passages, two from Ignatius and two from Polycarp. None of them follows the precise arrangement of 1 Timothy 3: 16: but they have the same two-element balance and expound the same truths. The first quotation from Polycarp may be based on 1 Peter 3: 18 ff.; there are four quotations from 1 Peter in the first two sections. But on the other hand, in section III Polycarp speaks of the 'blessed and glorious Paul', who taught firmly and accurately the meaning of truth in his letters, '. . . into which if you look carefully you will be able to build upon the faith (*pistis*) which was given to you; "which is the mother of us all".'

A mother is a person who gives birth: the faith in baptism gives the new birth in Christ; hence the rather unexpected quotation from Galatians (4: 26). The *homologia* is the expression of the Mystery, which is Christ, who is the Church, which is the 'mother of us all': by baptismal confession we are born into that Church. It is clear at least that Polycarp has baptism, and the confession of faith at baptism, in mind: it would be surprising if he did not include somewhere in his letter the substance of that confession. Perhaps it is the quotation from section II.

As he hints at his meaning in this, so also he hints at his meaning in the second quotation: deacons are told to 'walk according to the *truth of the Lord*'. What truth? What but the baptismal confession of the Church which is the pillar and stay of truth—and which is quoted in 1 Timothy 3: 16, *immediately after a section about deacons?*

In Ignatius and Polycarp the *homologia* pattern existed side by side with an emerging historical pattern—which was gaining ground on account of Docetic other-worldliness.

An examination of the writings of Justin Martyr is unproductive of the whole pattern. We find a different climate of thought altogether. There was no doubt why Christ became incarnate: 'He was conceived according to the will of God the Father, for the sake of believing men and for the destruction of the demons.' Manifested in flesh—believed on in the world of men—seen of demons: but the balance is gone—the flesh and spirit pattern. Again and again we find these same things taught, but somehow the large-scale view has gone, and the focus has contracted: fallen angels are there, but the emphasis is upon their misbegotten brood, the demons. The dragon has indeed come down to earth, and the strategy of the war against him has degenerated into a number of small-scale operations.

Here is a characteristic passage ('Why are Christians relentlessly and unreasonably persecuted?'):

> It is because evil demons of old made apparitions, and defiled women and corrupted boys, and showed to men such horrors that men who did not use reason to judge what was done, but were governed by fear, became terrified, and not knowing that these were evil demons called them gods, and addressed each of them by name according as each demon styled himself (1st Apol., 5).

The old tradition of the fall of the angels is there and clearly set out. Justin was not unfaithful to his sources. He was unsystematic but conscientious.

> He (God) entrusted to angels the care of mankind and of all things under heaven, and ordered their array on those terms . . . [i.e. that they should look after them] . . . But the angels broke the bounds of their array, and were ensnared into confusion with mortal women, and begat children who were called demons. And they followed this up by making slaves of mankind, partly by magical writings, partly through terrors and reprisals which they occasioned (2nd Apol. 5. The 'magical writings' come from the Similitudes of Enoch).

Although the tradition of the cosmic disaster is there, it has lost its cosmic proportions. The *Christus Victor* doctrine has become a kind of mass-exorcism. The 'Mystery of godliness' (and Justin calls it a mystery) has lost its magnificent sense of the sacramental.

The fault here lies not with the Gnostics, but with the Greek outlook. It was too fresh and unspoilt and innocent. Demons were not a disaster—they were dirt. The Greek attitude needed the mysticism of the Hermetists, as against the Babylonian magic of Posidonius or the secrets of the mystery cults, to mould it into something which could fit the cosmic pattern of the *homologia*. But Justin Martyr was a great man, and one who fitted the needs of his time and place: his service to the Church was immense.

The epistle to Diognetus, by an unknown author though once ascribed to Justin, is probably of the same date as the first Apology, except the last two sections which make up a second letter by a different hand and a little later: Lightfoot suggests Pantaenus as the author of the last two sections. I quote the passages from it in Lightfoot's translation, and page references are to the one volume edition (1893) of *The Apostolic Fathers* (italics are mine). The second letter begins:

> Mine are no strange discourses nor perverse questionings, but having been a disciple of apostles I come forward as *a teacher of the Gentiles*, ministering worthily to them, as they present themselves disciples of *the truth*, the lessons *which have been handed down*. For who that has been rightly taught and has entered into friendship with the Word does not seek to learn distinctly the lessons revealed openly to the disciples; (p. 510) [the translation is not quite that of Lightfoot here] to whom the Word was manifest, and spoke plainly though the unbelieving did not take it in; yet He explained them (the lessons) to disciples who had been reckoned faithful, and who learned through Him the mysteries of the Father, (or, learned the mysteries from the Father Himself). That is why He sent forth the Word to appear to Creation, who was dishonoured by the people, proclaimed by apostles, believed by nations.

There is the mention of *the truth*, and then later of mysteries. We have *manifest* (same Greek word as in the *homologia*), and then three phrases out of the four at the end are echoed from the *homologia*: they are disarranged, and they are all from the outward-and-visible side of the pattern—but in the Greek the three last phrases have the unmistakable and authentic ring. It can hardly be unconscious quotation or half-quotation: the avoidance of the inward-and-spiritual halves of the pairs seems deliberate, perhaps only because the author was emphasizing the visible side of revelation, perhaps because the mystery learned by disciples who had been reckoned faithful was not lightly to be broadcast in an open letter. If he had been willing to quote the *homologia* verbatim as from 1 Timothy, there seems to be no other good reason why he should not have done so: it would have fitted very well; there is a verbatim quotation in sec. 12 from 1 Corinthians 8: 1.

In the first letter (the early part of 'Diognetus') there may be a hint about the secrecy of the *homologia*. At the end of section 4, the author says that he considers Diognetus to have been sufficiently instructed in the rightness of Christian principles as against Jewish legalism and fussiness: '. . . but', he says, 'do not expect to be able to learn about the mystery of their own worship from man' (*theosebeias musterion*), p. 505.

In section 7, a magnificent passage deserves to be quoted in full, for it is surely the exposition of the very *homologia* which we are examining: I have, however, omitted passages where possible, and put in italics those words which may have come from the *homologia* or from 1 Timothy 3: 15, which introduces it, as well as such words as may suggest that he is expounding a form of creed (Lightfoot's Translation, p. 507):

> For it is no earthly discovery which *was committed* to them, neither do they care to guard so carefully any mortal invention, nor have they entrusted to them the dispensation of human *mysteries*. But truly the Almighty Creator of the universe, the invisible God Himself from Heaven, planted among men *the truth* and the holy teaching which surpasseth the wit of man, and fixed it firmly in their hearts, not as any man might imagine, by sending (to mankind) a subaltern or *angel*, or *ruler* [*archonta*—perhaps echoing Rom. 8: 38, archai, usually translated 'principalities', suggesting guardianship of nations], or one of those that direct the affairs of earth, or one of those who have been entrusted with the dispensations in heaven, but the very Artificer and Creator of the universe Himself by whom He made the heavens, by whom He enclosed the sea in its proper bounds, whose *mysteries* all the elements *faithfully* observe (*hou ta musteria pistōs panta phulassei ta stoicheia* . . .) . . . [here follows a catalogue of all things in heaven, earth and the abyss, which serve Him] . . . Him He sent unto them . . . (not to inspire terror) . . . in gentleness and meekness has He sent Him, as a king might send his son who is a king. He sent Him as sending God; He sent Him as (a man) unto men; He sent Him as *Saviour* as *using persuasion, not force* (*peithōn*, a verb which in the passive means *believe*): for force is no attribute of God. He sent Him as summoning, not persecuting; He sent Him as loving, not judging. For He *will send Him in judgment*, and who shall endure His presence?

Another possible reflection is in section VIII, 9–11:

> . . . having conceived a great and unutterable scheme, He com-
> municated it to His Son alone. For so long as He kept and guarded
> His wise design as *a mystery*, He seemed to neglect us and be care-
> less about us. But when He revealed it through His beloved Son,
> and *manifested* the purpose which He had prepared from the begin-
> ning, He gave us all these gifts at once, participation in His bene-
> fits, and sight and understanding (of mysteries) which none of us
> ever would have expected.

The *mustēria Theou* are again mentioned in X, 7, but without
any particular association of ideas significant for the *homologia*.

Now the author of sections I–X seems to have known the
Pauline corpus. Apart from our own 1 Timothy 3: 16, he half
quotes from the letters from St. Paul five times: he is not fond
of verbatim quotations. We cannot therefore argue for the
secrecy of the *homologia*, from his avoidance of verbatim quotation of it in his references. A dispassionate reading of the quoted
reference does, however, suggest that the *homologia* was to him
something more than merely a quotation from the Pastoral
epistles. The 'mysteries' were things observed (or perhaps
'guarded', 'kept safe', even 'kept secret') faithfully by the elements: God's own wise design was 'kept and guarded as a
mystery': its revelation was in Christ seen as 'saving', and revealed in a sense which A. N. Whitehead would have approved,
who said: 'The creation of the world—that is to say, the world
of civilised order—is the victory of persuasion over force.'[3] This
is something which belongs to the essence of God Himself: it is
not *an* idea in the Creative Mind, belonging only indirectly to
God through some super-Being set over the world. It is *the
Truth, the holy meaning* (*logos*), committed to men (*paredothē*
which in itself suggests a form of belief). It is to be learnt only
from God. And in the two sections appended to this letter to
Diognetus: '. . . the truth, the lessons which have been handed
down . . . revealed openly to the disciples' are expounded in
words and phrases which are unmistakably reminiscent of the
homologia.

It is likely that the author knew the *homologia* as a confession
of faith in its own right: at least he knew its pattern and teaching, which is what really matters. Ignatius also knew it, though

his preoccupations were different. Polycarp also knew something very like it. What of Irenaeus?

Irenaeus represents both East and West. In 'The Apostolic
Preaching' (section 3, p. 72), he speaks of baptism. He testifies
to the use of the threefold invocation, but adds a short flesh-and-
spirit parenthesis about Jesus Christ,

> 'And in the Name of Jesus Christ,   the son of God,
> Who was incarnate and died,   and rose again.'

He continues with a rather confused exposition of baptism, due
partly to his preoccupation with heretical Demiurge doctrines,
and partly to the Armenian translator from the Greek. But
apart from this, there is no trace either there, or in the exposition of the Teaching which follows, of the pattern of the *homologia*. There are flesh and spirit antitheses, the death-resurrection pattern. There is, as one would expect in Irenaeus, clear
teaching on Christ's subjection of the apostatizing angels, and
of a kind of pre-cosmic fall. There is much about sending the
gospel to the nations. The clauses are all there, but they are not
linked up into a pattern.

The summing up of all things in Christ was the centre of his
doctrine. One might suppose that a creed of Christ the Mystery
would be just what he wanted. But there were three things
about it which must have frightened him off: first that it was
the Mystery, and Gnostics had ruined that word. Irenaeus was
very much opposed to anything which suggested a secret tradition, and his whole great work against heresies was directed
against Gnostics who claimed to possess one (*contra* Haer. *passim*, e.g. Bk. III, 12, 13, 14; P.G. 7, pp. 892 ff.). The second was
the pattern of balanced pairs, which had been exploited by
many of the Gnostics, especially Valentinus and Basilides.

The third was Irenaeus' own profound suspicion of angels.
Just as the Docetists drove Ignatius to the factual creed (Smyrn.,
IX), because the danger which he was facing from that side was
an over-spiritualized and phantasmal Christ, so the Valentinians drove Irenaeus into suspicion of angels. He opposed the
idea of angels as creators, or pro-creators under God (*c*. Haer.
II, 2, 1–3, P.G. 7, p. 714). He briefly dismisses the commission
given to the archangel after Creation, to care for the world, by
calling him 'the steward', and his angels 'servants' (Ap. Preach-

ing, tr. A. Robinson, p. 81). He would be disinclined to enlarge
on the function of the angels as national guardians, though he
knew of it and quoted the Septuagint version of Deuteronomy
32: 8, to shew that the commission once given to angels was now
abrogated (*c.* Haer. III, 12, 9, p. 903).

The Alexandrines met the challenge of Gnosticism by seeing
what was good in it, and building on that. They refused to be
frightened away from what was valuable and good by those
who had perverted it. Irenaeus, himself an Eastern but an
adopted son of the West, knew of doctrines which he thought
too dangerous to teach: and in the West, the angels slowly lost
caste, until by the time of Lactantius they had become something of a liability even to their charges. Rome was particularly
vulnerable to the hysterical occultism of the Middle East, and
there was no doubt good reason for the cautious sifting out of
anything which distracted Christians from the solid and historical faith: but we Anglicans are in little danger from an over-
supernaturalist approach: we are already far too matter-of-fact.

We have lost the true sacramental line, which was drawn not
between matter and spirit, between visible and invisible, but
between perfect and imperfect, between creator and creature,
between 'angels who at first were holy' and those who had
'broken their array'. The *homologia* safeguards this pattern of
thinking.

The absence of any shadow of a reference either to the *homologia* itself or to its pattern, in Tertullian, must confirm us in
the view that its influence was dying in the second century: for
Tertullian's importance for the tracing of credal development is
without question. Much of the teaching contained in the *homologia* remained, in the West. Tertullian himself is a witness to
the importance attached to the restraint of evil powers, implied
in the two middle clauses of the *homologia*, and exercised through
various forms of exorcism. There were recurrences of interest in
it from time to time: and there was a growing, and almost unhealthy interest in the fallen angels, unhealthier in the West
than in the East—Lactantius and Commodianus being the
worst offenders (Instit. II, 9–16. Commod. Instr. 3).

Origen refers to the last clause in his treatise against Celsus
(III, 31). Hippolytus says God was manifested in 'body' (adv.

Noetum, 17); and he refers to the restoration of the heavenly orders by the 'mystery of his Incarnation' (Hipp. P.G. 10, p. 833).

Pseudo-Dionysius of Alexandria (the letter is almost certainly spurious) quotes the *homologia* to Paul of Samosata. Athanasius, in his fourth letter to Serapion (sec. 15. P.G. 26, p. 657), discusses the difficulty of reconciling the divine and human natures of Christ; and what is almost certainly a marginal gloss adds the words: '. . . they have the apostle keeping the two in agreement for them, and as it were his hand stretched out to them, in the saying, Great is the mystery of godliness, God [*sic*] was manifested in flesh.'

Why should this particularly obvious scriptural reference be made only in a marginal gloss? Why indeed should there be this studious avoidance of the text in all the Fathers from the end of the second century to the end of the fourth? Tertullian, Clement of Alexandria, Dionysius (unless the quoted letter be genuine), Cyprian, Athenagoras, Tatian, Minucius, Irenaeus, Athanasius, Origen, all avoid 1 Timothy 3: 16, as if it were a serpent. They quote freely from scripture, and particularly freely from the Pastorals. Origen in his commentary on St. John's Gospel, quotes the previous verse three times. But that verse is never quoted. And yet it is an obvious quotation, and would often fit the subject like a glove. The only reason can be the one we have suggested.

There, then, is the passing of a creed—as a creed. But the matter cannot be left there. Chapter 4 shewed how Chrysostom returned to the *homologia*—and later Photius: and in this chapter I have quoted a marginal gloss on Athanasius and a spurious letter of Dionysius of Alexandria. But there were others, Theodoret, Oecumenius, St. John of Damascus, who discussed it at length. Gelasius used the *homologia* as a creed again.[4] But the emphasis had shifted as the centuries went on. There was no need to underline the supernatural element, and much need to keep out heresy. So we kept our historical and doctrinal creeds, and only in our central mystery, the Eucharist, have we preserved anything of the *homologia* pattern. And on that we are not yet permitted to unite.

This chapter may suitably end with a passage from the Apostolic Constitutions, which gave directions for preparation for baptism. It contains the three key ideas which appear in the introduction to our *homologia*—confession ('we confess that')—mystery ('great is the mystery')—godliness ('of godliness'). The bishop is to

. . . consecrate the oil *in the Name* of the Lord Jesus, and give spiritual grace (first *homologia* pair). . . .
energy and power, forgiveness of sins (second *homologia* pair).
and preparation for the baptismal *confession* (believed on); so that the one anointed may be freed from all un*godliness* (*asebeia*) and become worthy of *initiation into the mystery* (*muēsis*) as commanded by the only-begotten (VII, 42).

In the sacramental pattern of the Church's worship, not in the Eucharist alone, the two-element balance remained—even if it was lost in the creeds which accompanied the sacraments.

NOTES

[1] O. Cullmann, *Earliest Christian Confessions*, p. 60 and footnote.
[2] See also Dr. Kelly's remarks on the Ephesian text; *Early Christian Creeds*, p. 69 f.
[3] A. N. Whitehead, *Adventures of Ideas*; the closing words of Chapter II and the theme of the whole chapter.
[4] John Berriman, in his *Critical Dissertation on 1 Tim. 3: 16*, (*vide* bibliography) gives this reference, which I have not verified: Gelasius, Hist. Concil. Nicaen., Lib. 2, cap. 23, apud Labb and Coffart, Tom 2, col. 217. Vid. etiam edit. Balfor., p. 152. 'The church of God', says he [Gelasius], 'has received the Holy and Apostolick Faith, not of Men, nor by Men, but from God, and the Saviour of us all Jesus Christ, the Son of the Living God; who (according to the dispensation of His Coming in the Flesh, a great Mystery of Godliness as it is written) was manifest in the Flesh and seen of Angels' (*ap' autou tou pantōn hemōn soterŏs kai Theou Iesou Christou tou huiou tou Theou tōu zontŏs: hŏs—phanerōtheis tĕ sarki kai angelois ŏphtheis*).
It is from John Berriman, I think, that I got the story of Gelasius using 1 Tim. 3: 16, as his creed in private devotions.
This dissertation of Berriman's is chiefly concerned to establish the reading *THEOS*, as against *HOS* or *HO*, at the beginning of the *homologia*. It is a careful and interesting study, without the MSS. at his disposal which have established the reading *HOS* almost beyond dispute. On the *durior lectio* principle anyhow *HOS* would be preferred.
Berriman also quoted the following fathers as support for his argument:

Arnobius junior (2nd book of conflict with Serapion), quotes Nestorius as reading '*HO ephanerothe en sarki*'; *vide* Cassian, *de Incarnatione Christi, contra Nestorium*; also pseudo-Chrysostom, *in Incarnationem Domini nostri Jesu Christi* (Chrys. opp. ed. Benedict., p. 213). Two references by Athanasius are almost certainly spurious: 4th ep. to Serapion, 15 (Ath. opera. ed. Benedict, Paris 1698, vol. 2, p. 706; also *vide* P.G. 26, p. 657) and De Incarnatione (vol. 3, p. 564). Four references are from Gregory of Nyssa: Tom. 2, Orat. 2, p. 430; Orat. 4, p. 536; Orat. 4, p. 581; Orat. 5, p. 595 (edit. Paris, 1638).

I have, I believe, verified these references in the editions quoted, but have not included them in the general list of patristic references, since they are not material to my theme. They all come from the period of renewed interest in the *homologia*, when Gnosticism had ceased to be a bogey.

Chapter 17

THE POEM OF THE INCARNATE WILL

My meat, said Jesus, is to do the will of Him that sent me (John 4: 34): this was what gave him life and maintained the physical body at a spiritual level, so that he remained the pattern of that Will.

Disciples are not themselves perfect, but they press continually towards the mark for the prize of the high calling of God in Christ Jesus. They live not directly on the meat which is the Will of God, but on the pattern of that Will manifested in flesh:

> I am the living bread which came from heaven: if any man eat of this bread he shall live for ever: and the bread that I will give is my flesh, which I will give for the life of the world.
>
> He that eateth my flesh and drinketh my blood, dwelleth in me, and I in him.

Jesus lived by direct and unbroken contact with the Will of God: our contact is with the pattern of the Will—a Mystery of what the Greeks called *Eusebeia*—manifested in flesh, justified in spirit.

The works of Jesus as Christ shewed the power of that Will over subconscious individual forces, and over the great archetypal ideas which had become demonic: the power extended to the racial unconscious—He was seen of angels, proclaimed among nations. The Will proclaimed in a creation which included forces both superhuman and inhuman gave stability in a universe of flux; fear and anxiety were exorcized where He was believed on in creation: the craving for beauty, for recognition, for glory was not left to burn unsatisfied, but found its satisfaction in the final revelation of a purpose, desire and will, which is beauty at its most perfect. He was received up in glory.

Through Christ alone, the Mystery of Eusebeia, is the way safe to knowledge of God. The Holy Ghost is the guide along that way for those who have not known Christ in the flesh: indeed, knowledge of Christ in the flesh may be an obstacle—as St. Paul suggests—to a grasp of truth (a warning to the Jesus-of-history school of thought). Truth, so reached in Christ through the Holy Ghost, is truth about God the Father. Such knowledge of truth about God is knowledge of Him as a Will—and indeed how else can we know Him? And how can we find anything more relevant than His Will for us men and for our salvation—a Will expressed in terms of *Eusebeia* with power and glory, penetrating to our own roots of action through the Holy Ghost.

It is because we have used wrong methods of approach to truth—prosaic methods, logical methods, occult methods—that we have quarrelled about doctrine and become divided.

Athanasius cannot be accused of indifference to heretical interpretation, yet we are told that he was:

> . . . not only a profound theologian, but was also willing to sacrifice all but the barest essentials of theological terminology so long as he was satisfied that the parties with whom he had to deal accepted the substance of the faith (G. L. Prestige, *God in Patristic Thought*, p. 186).

This quotation follows a story, in which Athanasius approved as orthodox both of two contending parties; the first confessed God in three *hypostaseis*, the second spoke of God in a single *hypostasis*. On another occasion he approved as orthodox some who confessed God in three *ousiai*, interpreting the term in the sense normally given to *hypostasis*.

Heretical belief must be shut out, but the Church has made heretics where there were none before with her categories and her definitions, many of them drawn from Greek philosophy instead of the revelation given in Christ. The poetic approach of Plato, reduced to the prosaic system of Aristotle, produced an alien God, chilly and aloof, impassible, untouched by human prayers, irrelevant to man. When Christians followed the Greeks in accepting arguments about what God *must be*, they were forgetting that we have in Christ a different picture—a picture of what He in fact *is*.

Equally the Church has gone wrong in trying to know *about*

the Holy Ghost, whose function is not to *be known about* but to mediate truth about the Will of God—whether incarnate in Jesus Christ or immanent in Christian hearts.

So the Church has fallen into strange doctrinal snares. We have asked questions which should not have been asked and can never be answered in human language—not because they were blasphemous but because they had no meaning. So, sometimes, unpoetic souls ask for the imagery of a poem to be explained; or, on a lower level, a dull listener demands to know the meaning of a joke. Not poetry, nor jokes, nor creeds can be explained to a mind—if there is one—which travels only in the canals of rational conscious thought. 'Is the Son subordinate to the Father?' 'By what authority—and who gave thee this authority?' 'What is the relationship of the Holy Ghost to the Father and the Son?'

Christ is the Mystery of the Will of God—and the mystery-creed sets the pattern out in six lines of poetry. This pattern was at the back of the books and speeches of the New Testament before there was a creed-pattern. The poetic pattern continued in the writings of early fathers, until angels and mysteries fell into disrepute through Gnostic misuse and exaggeration. But its doctrines—disjointed and with rhythm and balance lost —continued to be taught long after the 'Mystery of godliness' itself was banished.

Some may feel that—poetry or no poetry—the description of Christ as the Incarnate Will of God is a form of Arianism, or at least Adoptionism. Heretical labels are not important, except for convenience of reference; but this is neither Arian nor Adoptionist. What makes a person into a person? His *will*, which, through a series of decisions, shews that he is a person; for decisions build up personal existence. The efficacy of those decisions is their justification—their mastery of what is evil, their universal validity, their solid security, their satisfaction of the sense of beauty or fitness. *The Will of God is God*, as far as man is concerned, in mercy, in power, in unlimited scope, in rock-like reliability, in glory; and the Mystery of that Will is Christ, first as Creative Word:

(1) Let there be light—*manifested in flesh*—that which maketh manifest is light.

(2) Let there be a firmament . . . and God called the firmament heaven—*justified in spirit,* of which the other name is heaven—for spirit is the justification of flesh, and heaven the justification of earth.

(3) The separation of earth and waters—the redemption of the life-bearing soil from the waters of the abyss, the home of demons and monsters—*seen of angels* both fallen and unfallen, who bore witness to the beginning of redemption.

(4) Let there be lights in the firmament . . . for signs and for seasons and for days and for years—the greater light for God's own portion, Israel, and the lesser lights divided as the nations were divided 'according to the number of the angels of God'. The greater light was now at last to be seen by the people who walked in darkness, in Galilee of *the nations.*

(5) The creation of living creatures of the waters, of the atmosphere—*moving* creatures whom God blessed and commanded to multiply—bringing a new order of life into the elements which surrounded and enveloped the redeemed earth, but which were not yet quite of the earth—*the redemption of kosmos.*

(6) The living creature after its kind springing from the redeemed earth, which was now on its way to God and Life— fulfilled finally in the First Man, after God's own image and likeness, having dominion over every living thing—finally after many vicissitudes reintegrated in Jesus Christ, *received up in glory.*

The Mystery of the Will of God is, second, the Saving Word, who speaks to men most of whom are unconscious of any need of salvation. They are conscious of certain needs, or at least prepared to admit them when they are pointed out: but in these days they are tolerably sure that the Christian creed does not satisfy even those. Man demands that he shall wonder—and search, that he shall know truth, that he shall exercise power, that he shall have as great a share of opportunity as his neighbour, that he shall feel secure, that he shall win glory.

(1) The sense of wonder is akin to worship and is most healthily expressed in it. In natural religion this may not get

beyond hero-worship; but it is met at that point by Christ *the Mystery*.

(2) Man feels himself too often misunderstood. In this he is right; we are all mysteries to each other. Perhaps this is why misunderstood heroes have so great an appeal; we identify ourselves with them in their misunderstoodness. But the play or book which ends on a note of misunderstanding is unlikely to be a best seller. Misunderstanding must end in justification; Gareth must be recognized by Linet as the knight he is. Man knows himself to be better than he always seems to be—at least he wishes to know himself so, and be vindicated as such. He achieves vindication in Jesus Christ, the Incarnate Will of God, *manifested in flesh—justified in spirit*.

(3) The child's reaction to the miracles of the gospel is often, 'If only I could do what Jesus did!' In that sort of reaction many of us are still children; we want the power to do the work which Jesus did. Our own work seems full of obstacles, it is demon-possessed. We need a mediator to shew us the source of power, without which our highest achievements turn to dust and ashes. All pre-Christian mediators were and are unreliable and unpredictable, as dangerous as the dangers they avert. We need a mediator whose strength and goodness are both beyond question—whose control over the powers whom we fear has been demonstrated. That mediator we find in the victorious Christ, *seen of angels*.

(4) But we strongly suspect favouritism. We always do. We want our rights. Why should Jews have been chosen, and not the far more attractive Gentiles? Why should I have to belong to an exclusive organization called the Church? Down with institutional religion! But the Church is not exclusive: the barriers went down when Christ was *proclaimed among nations*. All that is asked of us is that we shall be humble enough to enter it. Whatever church may be exclusive, the Church of Christ is not. We can enter; we shall all have our rights in this age, and probably something more than our rights. We also inherit a promise.

(5) How then can we safely attach ourselves to Christ? Simply by abandoning fear and trusting Him. No more than that. When *creation believes on* Christ as Lord, it is at once redeemed.

L

(6) But—dare we say it?—we want more than all this. We are more than mere inquisitive seekers, more than power-lovers crying at the same time for security. We want recognition of ourselves for what we *really are* by someone who *really understands*. We want to be known, not as the miserable failures which this world has made of us, but as our true selves—the selves we might have been. We seek, in fact, to be *received up in the glory* of Jesus Christ our Lord, who alone can assess every man—and who will assess him, if he has faith, as the self he seeks to be and might have been and (in Christ) is. For this is the end of the Will of God for every created soul.

The whole pattern of creation and redemption, from Genesis to Revelation, is nicely calculated to the needs of men. It is constant to those needs, however varying its expression. We shall satisfy those needs neither by an unwarrantable escapism, nor by a pedestrian refusal to face the supernatural. Our many inventions are of no avail. Man without God cannot find God.

If it is too late to alter the pattern of our thinking, we can at least relate our thinking to a gospel which makes sense. We may feel little relish at first for the sense it makes: at least we shall have faced the truth. And the truth is that there is no divorce of flesh and spirit without disaster: flesh without spirit dies: spirit (for fallen beings) without flesh and form is a horror of unrestricted freedom, for which we are not fit.

We cannot make our own meanings. God gave us meaning, and apart from that meaning we do not in any real sense exist. Our meaning is His meaning, our form is His form, our thought His thought; or if it is not, His answer to our thought can only be 'No'. Our relation to God determines not only what we are, but whether we are: that same relation is determined by the pattern of our faith.

In this book I have searched not so much for a creed as for a true rhythm. The creed was there in the Bible, recognized as a creed—or more often as a fragment. I have tried to shew that it is no fragment, but rather a pattern which goes down beyond the roots of thought.

For me it has been an essay in detection. The pattern of the Mystery fitted something in me which was neither mine by nature nor mine by appropriation. The more I thought of it the more my inner chaos became resolved: the more I dwelt upon the pattern, the more sense seemed to be made of things both new and old—from the patriarchs to the Universe of Mr. Hoyle—from the miracles of the Old and New Testaments to the experiments of Professor Rhine.

I do not suggest that we shall find it easy to adjust ourselves to this ancient creed-pattern: but I do suggest that it is uncontroversial in the sense of being undenominational. It cuts across our divisions, whatever branch of the Church we may belong to. We may not like its supernaturalism because it is old-fashioned. We may not like its psychology because it is all too up-to-date. But I shall not disagree with this or that point in it because I am an Anglican: my friends will not disagree with that or the other because they are Roman, or Congregational, or Methodist.

It is all the more valuable because it is not a new concoction to suit all parties. It is not a compromise. Indeed I have claimed that it goes back beyond all our existing creeds, through the early faith of the Church of Christ, to the mind of Christ Himself.

BIBLIOGRAPHY

ANON, *A Mystery Which the Angels Desired to Look Into*, Quarto, London, 1647.

ANON, *The Mystery of Godlinesse: A general discourse of the reason that is in religion.*

ANON, *A Brief History of the Unitarians, called also Socinians, in four letters written to a friend*, 2nd ed., 1691.

AULEN, G., *Christus Victor*, S.P.C.K., tr. A. G. Herbert, 1931.

BABYLONIAN TALMUD, ed. Rabbi Dr. I. Epstein, 34 vols., Soncino Press, 1935–48.

BADCOCK, F., *The Pauline Epistles*, S.P.C.K., 1937.

BERDYAEV, NICOLAS, *Spirit and Reality*, Geoffrey Bles.

BERRIMAN, J., '*Theos ephanerothe en sarki*', *or a critical dissertation upon 1 Timothy 3: 16*, London, 1741.

BETHUNE-BAKER, J. F., *An introduction to the Early History of Christian Doctrine*, Methuen, 4th ed., 1929.

BLAIR, H. A., Articles 'Valentinus and the Arian Christ', *Ch. Quarterly Review*, No. 295, vol. CXLVIII; 'Two Reactions to Gnosticism', *Ch. Quarterly Review*, No. 304, vol. CLII.

BLAU, L., Article 'Sammael' in *Jewish Encyclop.*, vol. X.

BODKIN, M., *Studies of Type Images in Poetry, Religion and Philosophy*, O.U.P., 1951.

BOEHME, JACOB, transl. J. R. Earle, *On the Election of Grace*, Constable, 1930. *Dialogues on the Supersensual Life*, ed. Bernard Holland, London, 1901.

BRANDON, S. G. F., *The Fall of Jerusalem and the Christian Church*, S.P.C.K., 1951.

BURCKHARDT, J. G., *Dissert. inaug. vindiciae lectionis theos, 1 Timothy 3: 16*, e codice Alex. N.T. nuper a Wordio Londini edito. Leipzic, 1786, Quarto.

CHARLES, R. H., *Apocrypha and Pseudepigrapha of the Old Testament.* *The Book of Enoch*, O.U.P., 1912. *The Testament of the Twelve Patriarchs*, 1908.

CHAUNCY, C., *The Mystery Hid from Ages and Generations, etc.*, London, 1784, Octavo.

CLARK, LOWTHER, *The Use of the Septuagint in Acts*, from *Beginnings of Christianity*, vol. II.

COHEN, A., *Everyman's Talmud*, J. M. Dent, London; E. P. Dutton, New York, 1949.

CONYBEARE, F. C., 'The demonology of the New Testament': articles in *Jewish Quarterly Review*, vols. 8 and 9, 1896–7.

CREHAN, J., *Early Christian Baptism and the Creed*, Burns Oates.

CULLMANN, O., *Earliest Christian Confessions*, Lutterworth, 1949.
DODD, C. H., *The Apostolic Preaching and Its Developments*, Hodder and Stoughton, 1949.
According to the Scriptures, Nisbet, 1952.
DUNCAN JOHNSTONE and BLAIR, *Enquiry into the Constitution and Organisation of the Dagbon Kingdom*, Gold Coast Govt., 1932.
DUNNE, J. W., *An Experiment with Time*, 3rd. ed., Faber, 1934.
EATON, D., *The Mystery of Godliness Unfolded*, London, 1817.
ELIOT, T. S., *The Cocktail Party*, Faber.
The Idea of a Christian Society, Faber, 1939.
Selected Poems, Pelican.
EPSTEIN, I., *Babylonian Talmud*, q.v.
FARRER, A., *The Rebirth of Images*, Dacre Press, 1949.
A Study in St. Mark, Dacre Press, 1951.
FORMBY, C. W., *The Unveiling of the Fall*, Williams & Norgate, 1923.
FRAZER, J. G., *Folk-lore in the Old Testament*, vol. I, Macmillan.
The Golden Bough, Macmillan.
GINZBERG, L., *Talmud, of Jerusalem:* A commentary on the Palestinian Talmud, 1941.
Article in *Jewish Encyclop.*, vol. II, 'Asmodaeus, or Ashmedai'.
GOTTLOB, M., *Pauli epistula prima ad Tim. Graece, cum commentario perpetuo*, Lipsiae, 1837.
HARRISON, J. E., *Prolegomena to the Study of Greek Religion*, Cambridge, 1903.
HARRISON, P. N., *The Problem of the Pastoral Epistles*, O.U.P., 1921.
HORT, F. J., *The Christian Ecclesia*, Macmillan, 1908.
The Apocalypse of St. John, I–III, Macmillan, 1908.
HOSKYNS, SIR E., *The Fourth Gospel*, 2 vols., Faber, 1947.
JAMES, M. R., *The Apocryphal New Testament*, O.U.P., 1924.
JUNG, C. G., *Psychology and Alchemy*, Routledge & Kegan Paul, 1953.
Essays on Contemporary Events, Routledge & Kegan Paul.
KELLY, J. N. D., *Early Christian Creeds*, Longmans, 1950.
LAMPE, G. W. H., *The Seal of the Spirit*, Longmans, 1951.
LANGTON, E., *The Essentials of Demonology*, Epworth, 1949.
LAYARD, JOHN, *The Lady of the Hare*, Faber, 1945.
LEWIS, C. S., *Transposition and Other Addresses*, G. Bles, 1949.
Miracles, G. Bles, 1947.
LIGHTFOOT, J. B., *The Apostolic Fathers*. One volume edition. Macmillan, 1893.
The Macmillan commentaries under his authorship on Galatians, Philippians and Colossians.
LIGHTFOOT, R. H., *The Gospel Message of St. Mark*, O.U.P., 1950.
LOCK, W., *The Pastoral Epistles*, I.C.C., T. & T. Clark, 1936.
MACLEAR, G. F., *An Introduction to the Creeds*, Macmillan, 1909.
MANSEL, H. L., *The Gnostic Heresies*, John Murray, 1875.
MANSON, T. W., *The Sayings of Jesus*, S.C.M. Press, 1950.
MATTHEWS, W. R., *The Problem of Christ in the Twentieth Century*, O.U.P., 1951.

MELANCHTHON, PH., *Enarratio Ep. I ad Tim., et 2 cap. II*, Wittenburg, 1561.

Midrash Rabbah, ed. H. Freedman and M. Simon, Soncino Press, 1939.

MOFFATT, J., *Introduction to the Literature of the New Testament*, T. and T. Clark, 1911.

MOULTON and GEDEN, *Greek Concordance of the New Testament*, 3rd edition (reprinted) 1950, T. & T. Clark.

MURRAY, Gilbert, *Five Stages of Greek Religion*, O.U.P., 1930.

NEWBIGIN, LESSLIE, *The Household of God*, S.C.M. Press, 1953.

OESTERLEY and ROBINSON, *Hebrew Religion*, S.P.C.K., 2nd ed., 1937.

An Introduction to the Books of the Old Testament, S.P.C.K., 1937 (reprinted).

OULTON, J. E. L., *Credal Statements of St. Patrick*, as contained in the fourth chapter of his confession, Dublin, 1940.

OXFORD SOCIETY OF HISTORICAL THEOLOGY, Abstract of proceedings, 1948–9. Article by H. F. D. Sparkes, *q.v.*

PARRY, R. S. J., *The Pastoral Epistles*, Cambridge, 1920.

PHILO, *De Gigantibus*, transl. Colson & Whitaker, 1929.

Pistis Sophia. Transl. from Coptic, George Horner, S.P.C.K., 1924.

PLUMMER, A., *St. Luke*, I.C.C., T. & T. Clark, 1898, 2nd ed.

PRESTIGE, G. L., *God in Patristic Thought*, S.P.C.K., 1952.

RAMSEY, A. M., *The Resurrection of Christ*, G. Bles, 2nd ed., 1946.

The Glory of God and the Transfiguration of Christ, Longmans, 1949.

RAWLINSON, A. E. J., *The Gospel According to St. Mark*, Methuen, 1925.

RHINE, J. B., *The Reach of Mind*, Faber.

RICHARDSON, A. (ed.), *A Theological Word Book of the Bible*, S.C.M. Press, 1950.

RICHMOND, W. J., *The Creed in the Epistles*, Methuen, 1909.

ROBERTS, C. H., An unpublished fragment of the fourth gospel in the John Rylands Library, 1935, Manchester.

(With Dom B. Capelle), An early Euchologium: the Der-Balyzeh Papyrus, enlarged and re-edited, 1949, Louvain.

ROBINSON, H. WHEELER, *Inspiration and Revelation in the Old Testament*, O.U.P., 1946.

ROWLEY, H. H. (editor), *The Old Testament and Modern Study*, S.P.C.K.

SAURAT, DENIS, *Death and the Dreamer*, Westhouse, London, 1946.

SELWYN, E. G., *The First Epistle of St. Peter*, Macmillan, 1946.

SHEPHERD, A. P., *The Eternity of Time*, Hodder and Stoughton.

SOUTER, A., *Pocket Lexicon to the Greek New Testament*, O.U.P., 1920.

SPARKES, H. F. D., 'The Semitisms of Acts'. Paper given before the Oxford Society of Historical Theology, 1948–9. Abstr. of proceedings.

STREETER, B. H., *The Four Gospels*, Macmillan, 1924.

The Primitive Church, Macmillan, 1929.

Thinker, The, London, 1895, vol. 8. Articles by B. Whitefoord, *q.v.*

TORREY, C. F., *The Composition and Date of Acts*.

TURNER, C. H., *The History and Use of Creeds and Anathemas in the Early Centuries*, S.P.C.K., 1910.

WEATHERHEAD, L., *Psychology, Religion and Healing*, Hodder & Stoughton, 2nd ed., 1952.

WEBB, C. C. J., *Problems in the Relations of God and Man*, Nisbet, 1924. Reprinted.

WESTCOTT, B. F., Macmillan commentaries on the Gospel of St. John, the Epistles of St. John, and the Epistle to the Hebrews.

WHITE, VICTOR, *God and the Unconscious*, Harvill Press, 1953.

WHITE, N. J. D., *History of the Church of Ireland*, ed. W. A. Phillips.

WHITEFOORD, B., Article in *The Thinker*, vol. 8, No. 5, 1895: 'The Presence of a Creed in the New Testament'.

WHITEHEAD, A. N., *Adventures of Ideas*, Pelican.

WILLIAMS, Charles, *The Place of the Lion*, Gollancz, 1947.

WILLIAMS, N. P., *The Ideas of the Fall and Original Sin*, Longmans, 1927.

YEATS, W. B., *Collected Poems*, Macmillan, 1952.

PATRISTIC AND CLASSICAL REFERENCES

(P.L. and P.G. refer to the Latin and Greek series respectively of Migne's Patrologiae)

Chapter 1
Plinius minor opera. Teubner Edition: ed. R. C. Kukula (Lipsiae) 1923.
Letter 96 (97), Bk. X, p. 317.
(My own original reference was taken from the duodecimo edition of
Marcus Zuerius Boxhornius, Amstelaedami, ex officina Elzeviriana. 1659.
Ep. 97 of Bk. X.)
Chapter 2
Clement Alex. Stromateis VI, 15. P.G. 9, p. 348.
Augustine of Hippo. Ad Catechum. I, sec. 1. P.L. 40, p. 627 (*vide* p. 105.
C. A. Heurtley, De Fide et symbolo, Parker & Co., 1889, 4th edition).
Serm. CCXII, P.L. 38, pp. 1058, 1060.
Serm. CCXIV, P.L. 38, pp. 1065 f.
Tyrannius Rufinus of Aquileia. Comm. in Sybol. Apost., sec. 2, P.L. 21,
p. 338 B.
Jerome. contr. Joannem Hierosol: ad Pammachium, Bk. I, 28, P.L. 23,
p. 380.
Chapter 3
Irenaeus. contr. Haereseis, Bk. III, XXI, 4–10. P.G. 7, pp. 950–5.
Ignatius of Antioch. Ephes. XIX, Lightfoot Ap. Frs. (1 vol. ed.), pp. 110–
11.
Chapter 4
Irenaeus. c. Haer. II, XXVIII, 3. P.G. 7, pp. 805–6.
Eusebius of Caes. Hist. Eccles. Bk. III, 26, 4. P.G. 20, p. 272. And Bk. VII,
30, 16. P.G. 20, p. 716.
Chrysostom. Hom. in Past. Epp. in 1 Timothy 3: 16. P.G. 62, pp. 554–5.
Chapter 5
Lactantius. Div. Instit. II, 16. P.L. 6, pp. 335–6.
Photius. Ad Amphilochium, Q. XLIII, 13, 16. P.G. 101, pp. 320, 324.
Chapter 6
Athanasius. De Incarn. Text and notes, A. Robertson. D. Nutt, 270, Strand,
1882. All references in this chapter are to this edition.
Chapter 8
Chrysostom. Hom. in Past. Epp. P.G. 62, p. 554.
Theodoret. Commentary, on 1 Timothy 3: 16. P.G. 82, pp. 809 f.
Justin Martyr. 1st Apol. 5. P.G. 6, p. 336.
Tatian. Oratio ad Graec. XVII. P.G. 6, pp. 341 ff.

Papias. Fragment from Andreas Caesariensis, in Apocalypse in c. 34, serm. 12. Lightfoot, Ap. Frs., p. 521.

Polycarp. Ep. Phil. II, 1. Lightfoot, Ap. Frs., p. 168.

Ignatius. Ep. Trall. IX, 1. Lightfoot, Ap. Frs., p. 118.

Novatian. De Trin. 18, 19, 20. P.L. 3, pp. 918 ff.

Origen. c. Cels. I, 68. P.G. 11, p. 788.

   Hom. 7 in Exod. P.G. 12, pp. 341 ff.

   Hom. 27 in Num. P.G. 12, pp. 780 ff.

Tertull. Adv. Marc. IV, 24. P.L. 2, pp. 418 f.

Jerome. Ep. LXIX, 6. P.L. 22, pp. 659 f.

Chapter 9

Didache. In Lightfoot, Ap. Frs., pp. 217 ff.

Athanasius. Vita S. Anton. P.G. 26, pp. 877, etc.

Eusebius. Hist. Eccl. III, 39. P.G. 20, p. 296.

Chapter 10

Clement of Rome, c. 29. Lightfoot, Ap. Frs., pp. 20 f.

Hippolytus. contra Beronem et Helicem. P.G. 10, p. 833.

   in Psalm 24. P.G. 10, p. 609.

   in Sanct. Theoph. P.G. 10, p. 857.

Chapter 12

Clement, Recognitions; II, 71, 72. P.G. 1, pp. 1280 ff.

Justin Martyr. Dialogue with Trypho, LXXVI, 6. P.G. 6, pp. 652 ff.

   Ibid., LXXXV, 2. P.G. 6, pp. 676 ff.

   Ibid., CXXI, 3. P.G. 6, pp. 756 f.

   Ibid., XLIX, 8. P.G. 6, p. 585.

Minucius Felix. Octavius XXVII, P.L. 3, pp. 323 ff.

Tertullian. Apol. XXIII. P.L. 1, pp. 410 ff.

   Ibid., XXXVII. P.L. 1, pp. 461 ff.

   Ibid. XLIII. P.L. 1, pp. 495 ff.

   Ibid. XLVI. P.L. 1, pp. 500 ff.

Cyprian. Ad Demetr. 14, 15. P.L. 4, pp. 554–5.

Pseudo-Cyprian. De Grat. Dei, 5. Tauchnitz, ed. Goldhorn, 1838, Lipsiae.

Theophilus of Antioch. Ad Autolycum, Bk. II, 8. P.G. 6, p. 1062.

Lactantius. Div. Instit. II, 16. P.L. 6, pp. 335–6.

   Ibid. IV, 27. P.L. 6, pp. 531 ff.

Hippolytus. in Psalm 24. P.G. 10, p. 609.

Tyrannius Rufinus of Aquileia. Comm. in Symb. Apost. (Ascendit ad coelos), cap. 31. P.L. 21.

Tertullian. Scorp. 10. P.L. 2, pp. 141 ff.

Irenaeus. c. Haer. IV, 13. P.G. 7, pp. 1007 ff.

Chapter 14

Ignatius. Ep. Smyrn. V, VI. Lightfoot, Ap. Frs., pp. 128 f.

Polycarp. Ep. Phil. VII. Lightfoot, Ap. Frs., p. 171.

   Ibid., II, pp. 168 f.

Justin Martyr. Dial. c. Tryph. sec. 110. P.G. 6, p. 729.

   1st Apol. sec. 4. P.G. 6, p. 333.

   2nd Apol. sec. 2. P.G. 6, p. 445.

Pseudo-Ignatius. Philipp. III. P.G. 5, p. 924.

Clem. Alex., Strom. IV, 9. P.G. 8, pp. 1279–86.

Dionysius Alex. (in Euseb. H. E. VII, 8). P.G. 26, p. 813, Ic.

Justinian Imperat. adv. Orig. P.G. 86, p. 967.

Chapter 15

Tyrannius Rufinus. Comm. in Symb. Apost., sec. 2. P.L. 21, p. 337.

Justin Martyr. Dial. c. Tryph. 131. P.G. 6, p. 780.

Chapter 16

Ignatius. Ep. Trall. VIII, IX. Lightfoot, Ap. Frs., p. 118.

Polycarp. Ep. Phil. II, V. Lightfoot, Ap. Frs., pp. 168 ff.

Ep. Diognet. IV, VII, VIII, X, XI, XII. Lightfoot, Ap. Frs., pp. 492 ff.

Justin Martyr. 1st Apol. V, P.G. 6, p. 336.

    2nd Apol. V, P.G. 6, p. 452.

Irenaeus. 'The Apostolic Preaching', transl. A. Robinson, S.P.C.K.,
    pp. 72, 81.

    c. Haer. passim, in P.G. 7, espec. pp. 714, 892 ff., 903.

Lactantius. Div. Instit. II, 9–16. P.L. 6, pp. 293 ff.

Commodianus. Instruct. III. P.L. 5, pp. 203–4.

Origen. c. Cels. Bk. III, ch. 31. P.G. 11, p. 959 (ean de ho emos Iesous
    analambanesthai en doxe(i) legētai).

Hippolytus. adv. Noet. XVII. P.G. 10, pp. 826 ff.

    c. Beron. et Helic. P.G. 10, p. 833.

Dionysius of Alexandria (spurious) letter to Paul of Samosata. I have un-
    fortunately lost track of this reference: luckily it is not important to my
    argument. (It is, I believe, quoted by John Berriman, *A critical dis-
    sertation upon 1 Timothy 3: 16*.)

Athanasius. Ep. Serap. XV. P.G. 26, p. 657. London, 1741.

Apost. Const. VII, 42. P.G. 1, p. 1044.

APPENDIX

A Summary of References

A. The Guardians of the Nations
An Introduction to the Books of the Apocrypha, Oesterley, p. 108, quoting the
Targum to Genesis 11: 7 f. In this same place he mentions the three
most important O.T. passages on the subject.
Ecclesiasticus 17: 17.
Deuteronomy 32: 8 f., in the Septuagint.
Daniel 12: 1. And cf. Yalkut Shimeoni, Bereshith 132.
Psalm 2.
Isaiah 24: 21–3; *N.B.* especially the LXX translation of v. 23, with its sug-
gestion of the breaking down of barriers.
1 Enoch (R. H. Charles); chapters 89 and 90 suggest that the beast-angels
represent the nations.
Hebrew Religion, Oesterley and Robinson, pp. 389 f.
Essentials of Demonology, E. Langton, pp. 113 f., 163.
Inspiration and Revelation in the Old Testament, Wheeler Robinson, pp. 2, 145,
158, 170 footnote.
Mark 1: 12 f.; Luke 4: 1–13; Matt. 4: 1–11; accounts of Temptation.
Clem. Alex. Strom. VI, 17 (but for patristic reference in general, *v.* sub. C.
infra.).

B. Theriomorphic spirits, sometimes of nations, demonic or otherwise.
Genesis 3: the serpent archetype.
Leviticus 17: 7: for 'devils' read 'the Se'irim', i.e. the hairy ones.
Numbers 21: 6–8. The 'fiery serpents'.
Deuteronomy 8: 15. 'Fiery serpents and scorpions', of the desert.
2 Kings 23: 8. For 'the high places of the gates' read 'the high place of the
Se'irim'.
2 Chronicles 11: 15. For 'devils' read 'Se'irim'.
Isaiah 5: 29 f.; 11: 1–9; 13: 21; 14: 29; 24: 21–3; 30: 6; 34: 14.
Ezekiel 1: 5, 10; 8: 10; 10: 14.
Hosea 8: 5—and many other references to calf-worship.
Micah 7: 16 f. For worms read A.V. Mg. 'creeping things'.
Nahum 2: 11 ff. The nation of Assyria as a lion.
Zephaniah 2: 14. The 'beasts of the nations'.
Midrash Tehillim to Psalm 91: 5: 'There is a harmful spirit which flies like
a bird and shoots like an arrow'. Quoted in *Hebrew Religion*, Oesterley
and Robinson, p. 118. But the whole section on theriomorphic demons
should be read, pp. 111 ff.

Acts 11: 6. 1 Corinthians 15: 32, cf. Acts 19: 19. Romans 1: 23.

C. Some References to an Angelic Fall: 1st and 2nd century.

Luke 4: 5 f. Glory of kingdoms of world given to the devil.

   10: 17–20. Fall of Satan from heaven: subjection of spirits.

John 12: 31; 14: 30; 16: 11. Prince of this world.

1 Corinthians 6: 3. Men will judge angels.

   11: 10. Women to be covered for fear of angels.

2 Corinthians 11: 14. Satan an angel of light.

Ephesians 3: 1–12; 6: 12. Principalities, powers, world-rulers of darkness, spirits of wickedness in high places.

Philippians 2: 10. Subjection of things in heaven, earth, and under the earth.

Colossians 1: 20. Reconciliation of all things.

   2: 15. Spoiling of principalities and powers on the cross.

1 Peter 3: 18–22. Spirits in prison.

2 Peter 2: 4; and Jude 6. Fall of angels.

Revelation 12: 9–12. The devil and his angels cast out of heaven.

1 Clement XXIX (quoting Deuteronomy 32: 8 f., in Septuagint version).

Ignatius: Eph. 13, 17, 19. Magn. 1. Trall. 4, 5. Rom. 5, 7. Phil. 6. Smyrn. 6.

Didache 3 (dead gods), 16 (the world deceiver).

Barnabas 4: 13 (the evil archon); 18 (the two sets of angels).

Papias. Fragm. XI in Lightfoot App. Fathers, p. 521.

Justin Martyr. 2 Apol. IV (V), 2, 3; VI (VII), 1, 5. Dial. 7, 30, 45, 79, 83, 91; also 131 (quoting Deuteronomy 32: 8 f.—in LXX).

Tatian. Or. ad Graec. 100, 11A, B, 23B.

Theophilus. ad Autol. II, 28.

Athenagoras. Apol. 25.

Irenaeus. Epideixis, 11, 12. c. Haer. I, 10 (1, 3); III, 12 (29); IV, 6 (6 f.); and elsewhere.

Clement Alex: Strom. V, 13; Paed: III, 2 (14); Protr: I, 48.

Tertullian. De carne Chr: 14; de Orat: 22; de cult: fem: I, 2; and II, 10; Apol: XXXV, 12; de Idol: 9.

Lactantius. Instit. II, 9; and passim.

These references are only a few of the many. They shew that to the early Church the angelic fall belonged to the centre of Christian doctrine. The Atonement was indeed the restoration of the broken array, which had separated creation from its Creator. In this conception of the Atonement, Christian thought followed the Apocalyptic literature, and left the main stream of Jewish orthodoxy. *Vide Everyman's Talmud,* p. 54: 'The story of the fallen angels, which figures in Apocalyptic literature, is not found in Talmud or Midrash.'

This break away from Judaism proper, beginning probably from our Lord Himself and clearly embodied in the teaching of St. Paul, is surely of the utmost significance.

D. *Some Rabbinic References.* ((*a*) From Midrash Rabbah; ed. Rabbi Dr. H.
Freedman and Maurice Simon. Soncino Press, 1939.)

Vol. III, p. 126 and footnote (IX, 9): to Exodus 7: 16 f. (The heavenly
hosts are first punished, then the kings of nations under their control.)
(But cf. vol. VII, part II, p. 3, where hosts of heaven are interpreted as
their earthly governments.)

Vol. III, p. 411 f. (XXXII, 7): to Exodus 23: 20. (Angels of Jacob's dream
interpreted as spirits of nations.)

Vol. IV, p. 286 (XXII, 8): to Leviticus 17: 7. (He-goats are satyrs and
demons.)

Vol. V, pp. 451 ff. (XII, 3): to Numbers 7: 1. (In Psalm 91, 'terror', 'arrow',
'pestilence', 'destruction', interpreted as demons of night and day.)

Vol. VII, part I, pp. 24 f. (I, 22): to Deuteronomy 2: 31. ('God does not
exact punishment of any nation before He first exacts punishment of its
guardian angel'—the angel of Egypt was drowned first, i.e. 'The
horse', and then the army, i.e. 'his rider'.)

Vol. IX, part II, p. 326 (VIII, 14, 1): to Song of Songs.

(R. Hunia said with reference to the dictum of R. Isaac:

'The Holy One, blessed be He, does not punish a nation on earth till
He has cast down its guardian angel from heaven. This is borne out by
five scriptural verses. One, the verse:

"And it shall come to pass in that day, that the Lord shall punish the
host of the high ones that are in heaven on high"—

that first, and then—

"And the kings of the earth upon the earth" (Isaiah 24: 21).

The second is:

"How art thou fallen from heaven, O Lucifer, son of the morning"
(14: 12),

after which we read:

"How art thou cut down to the ground, which didst weaken the
nations".

The third is:

"For my sword shall be bathed in heaven" (34: 5)—

and then:

"Behold, it shall come down upon Edom."

The fourth:

"To bind their kings with chains" (Psalm 149: 8)—

and then:

"And their nobles with fetters of iron",

explaining which R. Tanhuma said: " 'To bind their kings with chains',
this refers to the heavenly princes; 'And their nobles with fetters of iron',
this refers to the earthly rulers."

The fifth is:

"To execute upon them the judgement written" (Psalm 149: 9)—

and then:

"He is the glory of all His saints, hallelujah".')

((*b*)) The following are references to the 'Seventy nations'.)

Vol. I, p. 319 (XXXIX, 11): to Genesis 12: 2.

Vol. IV, p. 22 (II, 8), also p. 26: to Leviticus 1: 2. (Seventy nations were originally created. Israel was chosen not for its righteousness, but for its acknowledgment of God.)

Vol. V, pp. 23 f., 267, 417 (Numbers).

Vol. VI, pp. 528, 806 (Numbers).

Vol. VII, part II, p. 95: to Lamentations 1: 2.

Vol. IX, part II, pp. 36, 91, 117 (Song of Songs).

(It may be pertinent here to refer to the theory of S. Mowinckel, on the New Year Festival, in which Yahweh in ritual drama 'triumphs over the kings and nations of the earth, who are allies of the primeval chaos . . .'. He uses some of the Psalms to make his case. *Vide The Old Testament and Modern Study*, p. 191.)

((*c*)) From the Babylonian Talmud: ed. Rabbi Dr. I. Epstein. Soncino Press, 1935–48)

The seventy nations and their Guardians.

Mo'ed II, p. 420, Shabbath 88b. Exposition of Psalm 68: 12, 'The Lord giveth the word. They that publish the tidings are a great host.' The word that went forth from the Omnipotent was split into seventy languages. The school of R. Ishmael taught: ' "And like the hammer that breaketh the rock in pieces" (Jeremiah 23: 29)—just as a hammer (blow) is divided into many sparks, so every single word that went forth from the Holy One, blessed be He, split up into seventy languages.'

Mo'ed II, p. 421 ff., Shabbath 88b–89a. At the ascent of Moses to receive the Torah, the angels protested: Satan then tried to get possession of it; the angels were reconciled and Satan thwarted.

Mo'ed II, p. 588, Shabbath 119b. Every man has both a good and an evil angel.

Mo'ed V, p. 84, Yoma 19b. Angels have beast forms, as is shewn by the fate of the Sadducee who improperly offered incense and was struck by an angel: the mark of a calf's foot was found on his shoulder.

Mo'ed VIII, p. 176, Megillah 29a. The mountains Tabor and Carmel were represented by their angel Guardians at Sinai, when the Torah was given. (Fallen angels were said to have been covered by mountains in the Book of Enoch.)

Nashim VI, p. 162 f., Sotah 33a. Gabriel was exceptional among angels in knowing the seventy languages—including Aramaic. These seventy languages he taught to Joseph. The ministering angels do not understand Aramaic (presumably because they have not been divided and dispersed as were the fallen angel Guardians).

(*d*) *The seven heavens, and the Temptations of Christ.*

Mo'ed VIII, p. 71 ff., Hagigah 12b. The heavens are seven, according to Resh Lakish, namely *Wilon* (curtain) by which the work of creation is daily renewed;

Rakia' (firmament) which is the place of sun, moon and stars (here must be placed the heavenly Guardians, amongst the signs of the zodiac);

Shehakim (clouds, dust) where the heavenly bread is ground for the righteous;

Zebul (height, lofty abode) where the heavenly Jerusalem stands; this is the prototype of the earthly Jerusalem (cf. R. Johanan's saying, Taanith 5a, 'I will not enter the heavenly Jerusalem until I can enter the earthly Jerusalem', explaining Hosea 11: 9, translated, 'the Holy One in the midst of thee and I will not come into the city'): there Michael the great prince stands and offers up thereon an offering;

Ma'on (dwelling) holds companies of angelic ministers, silent by day but singing praise by night;

Makon (fixed place or foundation) is the place of snow, hail, rain and storm, the dwelling place of God (1 Kings 8: 39);

'Araboth (thick darkness?) holds righteousness and judgment, the spirits and souls of the unborn, and of the righteous departed; God rides upon this (Psalm 68: 5).

Is this picture of the seven heavens the background of the Temptation vision of our Lord, and of His exposition of it to His disciples?

The visionary ascends, after the discipline of fasting, to the third heaven (cf. 2 Corinthians 12: 2): this follows his refusal of miraculously made earthly bread, and it is therefore the logical conclusion of His refusal that He should find Himself in the place of heavenly bread (Shehakim).

Accepting St. Luke's order, He looks down from there upon the Guardians of the nations in the second heaven (the kingdoms of the world and the glory of them), or in St. Mark's terminology upon the 'wild beasts' (*theria*): He refuses this temptation, and so rises to the fourth heaven.

Here He is in the heavenly Jerusalem, and is tempted to descend from there as 'Son of Man' on clouds of glory, and so fulfil the Messianic prophecy: He refuses this temptation, and so rises to the fifth heaven.

In it He finds Himself amongst the companies of angel ministers, who minister to Him. (Elsewhere I have suggested that the ministering angels were the Guardians, fallen but redeemed. It is not important whether the one or the other be accepted.)

INDEX